PRAISE FOR
WHERE GOODNESS STILL GROWS

"If the church of your childhood has broken your heart—particularly, politically—if your faith foundations have been shaken by betrayal and complicity, it might seem quaint to turn toward virtues. And yet what are we yearning for but embodied goodness? Amy has given us a well-researched, beautifully written, strong book about the virtues necessary for the apocalypse. We need to lean in further to discernment, lament, love, and hospitality, not in a weak be nice sort of way but in the muscular, lean way that holds on to hope out of faith disguised as sheer stubbornness. This book is one part lament, one part hope, and entirely necessary for these days."

—SARAH BESSEY, AUTHOR, *MIRACLES AND OTHER REASONABLE THINGS* AND *JESUS FEMINIST*

"Readers will find [Peterson's] courageous exposure of American evangelicalism's watered-down version of Christianity eye-opening, convicting, refreshing, and inspiring."

—CAROLYN CUSTIS JAMES, AUTHOR, *FINDING GOD IN THE MARGINS* AND *MALESTROM*

"In this poignant, honest book, Amy Peterson confronts her disappointment with the evangelical leaders who handed her *The Book of Virtues* then happily ignored them for the sake of political power. But instead of just walking away, Peterson rewrites the script, giving us an alternative book of virtues needed in this moment. And it's no mistake that it ends with hope."

—JAMES K. A. SMITH, AUTHOR, *YOU ARE WHAT YOU LOVE*,
AND EDITOR-IN-CHIEF, *IMAGE* JOURNAL

"Amy Peterson reflects the best of the church's next generation. With biblical faithfulness and wisdom, *Where Goodness Still Grows* gently critiques the shortcomings of the generation who came before her, then lovingly points the way toward a more holistic and virtuous future for all who claim the name of Christ."

—KAREN SWALLOW PRIOR, AUTHOR, *ON READING WELL* AND *FIERCE CONVICTIONS*

"Deconstructing is becoming a new normal; re-envisioning a path forward in the shadow of tradition is increasingly rare. Through gorgeous prose and widening her scope to a diverse array of voices, Peterson is doing the hardest work of all: stubbornly clinging to faith while holding it accountable at the exact same time. This book is vital reading."

—D. L. MAYFIELD, AUTHOR, *ASSIMILATE OR GO HOME*
AND *THE MYTH OF THE AMERICAN DREAM*

"Set against a culture where truth is for sale and faith trades down for power, this exquisite book invites us to abandon fear, cultivate curiosity, and learn to connect. If you're searching for signs of life, you will find them here."

—SHANNAN MARTIN, AUTHOR, *THE MINISTRY OF ORDINARY PLACES AND FALLING FREE*

"Amy Peterson's reflective, impassioned book is for anyone who, like me, both loves the evangelical Christian movement in which you were raised and also grieves its compromises and inconsistencies. It is one of the most genuinely hopeful books I've ever read: clear-eyed about Christian complicity in evil, resolute in its determination to recover the good in spite of the church's failures, and visionary in its attempt to imagine a better future."

—WESLEY HILL, AUTHOR, *SPIRITUAL FRIENDSHIP*

WHERE GOODNESS STILL GROWS

RECLAIMING VIRTUE IN AN AGE OF HYPOCRISY

AMY PETERSON

W PUBLISHING GROUP

AN IMPRINT OF THOMAS NELSON

Published in Nashville, Tennessee, by W Publishing Group, an imprint of Thomas Nelson.

Thomas Nelson titles may be purchased in bulk for educational, business, fund-raising, or sales promotional use. For information, please e-mail SpecialMarkets@ThomasNelson.com.

Unless otherwise noted, Scripture quotations are taken from the ESV® Bible (The Holy Bible, English Standard Version®). © 2001 by Crossway, a publishing ministry of Good News Publishers. Used by permission. All rights reserved.

Scripture quotations marked KJV are from the King James Version. Public domain.

Scripture quotations marked NIV are from the Holy Bible, New International Version®, NIV®. © 1973, 1978, 1984, 2011 by Biblica, Inc.® Used by permission of Zondervan. All rights reserved worldwide.

Scripture quotations marked NKJV are from the New King James Version®. © 1982 by Thomas Nelson. Used by permission. All rights reserved.

Scripture quotations marked THE MESSAGE are from *The Message*. © by Eugene H. Peterson 1993, 1994, 1995, 1996, 2000, 2001, 2002. Used by permission of NavPress. All rights reserved. Represented by Tyndale House Publishers, Inc.

Scripture quotations marked NRSV are from New Revised Standard Version Bible. © 1989 National Council of the Churches of Christ in the United States of America. Used by permission. All rights reserved.

Portions of chapter 3 were originally published in the author's work *Open Hearts, Open Homes*, as part of the Discovery Series, Our Daily Bread Ministries, 2017. Used by permission.

The author's essay "Basket Weaving," published at Patheos.com (blog), November 28, 2012, was adapted and incorporated into chapter 6. Used by permission.

The author's essay "What We Cannot Hold," published at *Art House America* (blog), June 18, 2016, was adapted and incorporated into chapter 7. Used by permission.

The author's essay "Chicken Eight Ways," published in *The Cresset*, Trinity, 2016, was adapted and incorporated into chapter 9. Used by permission.

978-0-7852-2573-7 (eBook)

Library of Congress Cataloging-in-Publication Data

Names: Peterson, Amy, 1981- author.
Title: Where goodness still grows : reclaiming virtue in an age of hypocrisy / Amy Peterson.
Description: Nashville : W Publishing Group, an Imprint of Thomas Nelson, 2020. | Includes bibliographical references. | Summary: "Where Goodness Still Grows dissects the moral code of American evangelicalism and puts it back together in a new way. Amy writes as someone intimately familiar with, fond of, and also deeply critical of the world of conservative evangelicalism. She writes as a woman and a mother, as someone invested in the future of humanity, and as someone who just needs to know how to teach her kids what it means to be good. She reimagines virtue as a tool, not a weapon; as wild, not tame; as embodied, not written. Reimagining specific virtues, such as kindness, purity, modesty, hospitality, and hope, Amy finds that if we listen harder and farther, we will find the places where goodness still grows"— Provided by publisher.
Identifiers: LCCN 2019032806 (print) | LCCN 2019032807 (ebook) |
  ISBN 9780785225669 (hardcover) | ISBN 9780785225737 (ebook)
Subjects: LCSH: Virtue. | Character. | Virtues. | Christian ethics.
Classification: LCC BV4630 .P465 2020 (print) | LCC BV4630 (ebook) | DDC 241/.4—dc23
LC record available at https://lccn.loc.gov/2019032806
LC ebook record available at https://lccn.loc.gov/2019032807

Printed in the United States of America

20 21 22 23 24 LSC 10 9 8 7 6 5 4 3 2 1

For Dad, whose love endures even when we disagree

CONTENTS

FOREWORD

I LOVE THE BOOK YOU'RE HOLDING. I HAVE READ IT FIVE TIMES AND WILL read it, I am sure, five times more.

What I should tell you about this book, I think—other than you will be charmed by and want to remain in the company of its narrator and will delight in the cunning and precise prose—is that where *Where Goodness Still Grows* sits in the tradition of what we might call—if we were using the lovely old-fashioned terms— moral theology. That is, where the book sits in the long tradition of Christian writers considering the life God wants for and expects of us, which, for Christians, is identical to the life in which we flourish.

In the literal sense, when I'm not reading it, *Where Goodness Still Grows* sits on my shelf next to books from the eighteenth and nineteenth centuries with titles such as *Moral and Instructive Tales for the Improvement of Young Ladies* and *Evening Amusements for the Ladies; or, Original Anecdotes Intended to Promote a Love of Virtue in Young Minds* (which are also books I love; they meditate topics like "Filial Duties" and "Humility," and they tell stories of characters like Miss Clara Haughty, a young girl who eventually allowed "goodness" to "triumph . . . over pride").

Where Goodness Still Grows sits next to those eighteenth- and nineteenth-century volumes because, like them, *Where Goodness Still Grows* understands that showing us what's entailed in being virtuous—what's entailed in being a flourishing human being—is a task that must be taken up every year or so, every generation. Virtues must always be, not reinvented but recast—melted down and reshaped—because new external circumstances (a war or an iPhone or a rising sea or Donald Trump) mean that Christians have to think again about the question "What's it like to be a human being alongside this?"—alongside iPhones and climate change. In *Where Goodness Still Grows*, Amy Peterson shows us what a life of virtue looks like in a world of empire, inequality, dislocation, sexual violence, movement of people groups. What was good for the young lady of 1848 is good for us, too, but those goodnesses need to be recast because so many of our particulars are different from Miss 1848's particulars.

I knew Amy during the months she was writing this book, and I think she thought the book's aim was centrally to explore and commend nine distinct virtues—purity, hospitality, and so forth. Those nine explorations and commendations are a central achievement of the book, but there's another achievement, too, one perhaps more foundational: Amy doesn't just model practicing hospitality and kindness. She also models a way of reading one's own past. In *Where Goodness Still Grows*, Amy Peterson's characteristic mode is to reconstrue. She picks up a virtue taught to her in childhood and sees it again in our context. She does not shy away from criticizing some of what was taught to her twenty-five years ago—castigating those earlier learnings for prizing bland compliance in women, for privileging seeming spontaneity over habitual performance of liturgical duty, for distorting the doctrine of providence into something that silenced the psalms of lament.

But, crucially, Amy does not wholly dismiss her childhood lessons. Rather, she's able to look back on the virtues she learned in childhood and see that those virtues were deformed but also always threaded through with goodness. And Amy has picked up those threads and woven a garment of virtue. So, yes, she shows us how to be kind and hospitable; but more fundamentally, she shows us how to read our own lives, our own childhoods and pasts and the communities that shaped us, with compassion and attentiveness. We each have, this book seems to say, a choice about how we look back on our past selves. We can look back on earlier seasons with nothing but bitterness, or, for that matter, we can look back on earlier seasons and imagine them, nostalgically, to have been unmixed bliss. But Amy shows us how to look back on our past selves and communities more truthfully, seeing both damage and beauty, and discriminating them. The ultimate work of *Where Goodness Still Grows* is not to teach us to think in a bolder, edgier way about kindness and hospitality. The ultimate work is to teach us how to read our pasts and then to turn to our present selves and communities and see there, too, a mixture of damage and beauty and to encourage us to move forward in the direction of the beauty, the good (even though, as Amy's first chapter—the lament chapter—acknowledges, we'll never be able to do so perfectly).

So this book wants to be read. And then it wants to be returned to your shelf; the next thing to read is your life, your past and your present, with as much compassion and clarity and incisiveness as Amy reads hers. And then *Where Goodness Still Grows* wants you to stop reading and go on with the rest of life, not merely with an intent to welcome more strangers or to love but rather to do those things *exactly because we've received from this book a deeper capacity to see around us the good and the bad all mixed up*—and having seen, we can respond, more than we could before Amy tutored us, with lament and kindness and hospitality and purity and modesty and authenticity and love and discernment and hope.

—LAUREN F. WINNER, associate professor,

Duke Divinity School

INTRODUCTION

VIRTUES FOR THE
APOCALYPSE

AROUND THE TIME THE LEAVES TURNED RED, MY APOCALYPSE BEGAN.

/3

I grew up on the margins of the moral majority, in a conservative evangelical homeschooling family in the South. You probably
have a picture of us in your mind now, one informed by reality
television; but if you had met us, you wouldn't have thought we
were weird, just maybe slightly outside of the mainstream. We
didn't wear denim jumpers we'd sewn ourselves (at least, not all
the time), or live in a commune, and there were only five children

in our family, not seventeen. We didn't totally kiss dating goodbye in favor of courtship, but the guys who wanted to take me out did have to call my father for permission first.

We memorized hymns and catechisms and Bible verses and went to church twice a week; we also played on community soccer teams and made friends at the neighborhood pool. Steven Curtis Chapman and Amy Grant and *Adventures in Odyssey* rotated through our tape deck, and while we avoided Madonna and MTV, we marinated in plenty of classic pop culture: albums by the Beatles and Joni Mitchell, movies starring Gene Kelly and Judy Garland, shows like *The Brady Brunch* and *I Love Lucy*. Our parents encouraged us to read widely, and to question everything. We never had any reason to doubt that we were deeply loved.

We weren't wildly political—we never stood in picket lines or marched on Washington or campaigned for candidates. Politics held little hope for us, as our faith was fixed instead on a heavenly future promised by God. But we did attend pro-life fund-raisers and boycott stores that donated to Planned Parenthood, and while we didn't talk much about it, it was clear to me as a child that the Republican Party was the party of family values and religious freedom, the party that would support the things we cared about, and that the Democrats weren't to be trusted. We knew that America was blessed by God, that abortion was our national sin, that anyone who tried hard enough would succeed, and that the law was basically fair. After all, it worked well for most people we knew.

When I was in my early teens, Dad would sometimes read to my four younger siblings and me as we finished our dinner.

As we diligently cleaned our plates, we would listen to a selection from our heavy hardback copy of *The Book of Virtues: A Treasury of Great Moral Stories*. The poems, fables, stories, and snatches of essays collected in the volume were written by a variety of mostly Western thinkers—Aesop and Plato, Hilaire Belloc and James Baldwin, Hans Christian Andersen and Isaac Watts. Our favorite—a piece we still quote today—was a poem about Augustus, who was a fat and ruddy lad until the day when he refused his dinner.

> O take the nasty soup away!
> I won't have any soup today.

The poem's humorous tone turns rather grim when, on his fifth day of refusing soup, Augustus died. Thus, we learned we ought to be grateful for the food on our plates. We scraped up the last bites, and we were.

The Book of Virtues was edited, with commentary, by conservative politician and pundit William J. Bennett, and published in 1993, when I was twelve years old. Bennett divided the book into ten thematic chapters: self-discipline, compassion, responsibility, friendship, work, courage, perseverance, honesty, loyalty, and faith. The book was bought and beloved by a wide swath of political conservatives, Christians, and homeschoolers, and it showed that morality was simple. There were good guys and bad guys. If you weren't grateful for your soup, you would die. If you didn't mind your parents, according to James Whitcomb Riley's "Little Orphan Annie," the goblins would get you. While *The Book of Virtues* wasn't deeply formational for me, like a pop song coming over the speakers at the grocery store, it evokes a certain era in my life, a time when the religious right was ascending, and represented a trustworthy arbiter of goodness.

My politics began to change during my twenties. After living overseas and on the West Coast, my perspective shifted, and I began to care about the environment and immigration and health care and the prison system. I lost confidence in the free market's ability to regulate itself. I began to see that racism was alive and well in the United States of America. But even as I began voting differently than my parents and many of the Christians I knew, I continued to believe in the good faith of those Christian leaders who supported Republican candidates. I trusted that their intentions were good, and that though we came to different conclusions, we both arrived at our conclusions out of a sincere desire to honor God in our political engagement.

In the past few years it has become more difficult to believe that.

During the 2016 election, the community that taught me that character counts, that truth exists, and that the ends do not justify the means threw its support behind a man who is a compulsive liar, a cheater, a racist, a misogynist, a narcissist, and a danger to the survival of democracy. As Donald Trump's campaign progressed, my dismay grew. I was shocked when he called Mexicans rapists and Christian conservatives said nothing. I was shocked when he said he wanted to close all mosques in America and again they said nothing. (Wasn't religious freedom one of their bywords?) I was shocked when he mocked a reporter with a physical disability and they stayed silent. I was shocked when no one thought his lies problematic, just par for the course. It shouldn't have taken me as long as it did—but the shock finally became revelatory for me when he turned to women's bodies. When that 2005 videotape was released in which Trump bragged about grabbing a woman by her "pussy" to get what he wanted from her and the only thing conservative religious leaders said was *locker room talk, people change,* and *we should forgive*—that was when they lost me.

In my formative childhood years my Christian faith and my understanding of virtue were tied to a set of political beliefs and a particular subculture in America. But now I had to wonder: Had anyone believed in the virtues they'd taught me? Or had those virtue claims always been weapons wielded to preserve power for the powerful and keep everyone else in place? This man bragged about infidelity and abuse, said he had nothing to repent of, and walked into women's dressing rooms at beauty pageants to ogle them, as if he owned them. The Christian culture that taught me about fidelity, modesty, and sexual purity stayed silent. It appeared that my woman's body was a pawn they were willing to play in the game for political power.

I had expected them to care about the way Trump treated women. After all, when I was a teenager, those religious leaders whose shadows loomed large in my life had been very vocal in their condemnation of Bill Clinton's marital infidelity. Again and again, though, the people who had spoken out against Clinton spoke forcefully in support of Trump. This hypocrisy wasn't just limited to evangelical leaders. Statistics show that Christians in general have grown dramatically more accepting of politicians' immoral behavior. In 2011, only 30 percent of evangelicals would forgive a president's immoral conduct; just five years later, 72 percent were willing to overlook it. What changed in those five years? Obama left office, and Trump ran for president.

꒰ꕤ꒱

Something has gone terribly wrong in the culture that taught me about virtue. I learned how to find truth in Scripture and orient my life around loving God and my neighbor from a community that seems to have stopped believing many of the things they taught me—things like the value of every human life, the importance of religious freedom, and the sanctity of marriage; things like hospitality, purity, modesty, truth, and love. I find myself now wondering if the ground I grew up in was radioactive all along and whether anything good can grow here. Does this hypocrisy mean I need to discard everything I learned growing up in the evangelical church?

I'm not sure I'm willing to do that. In church I learned the truths I still hold dearest: that I am created in the image of God, that I am worthy of love, and that I am, in fact, deeply loved. That I live in a world that needs rescue and repair, and that I, too, need rescue and repair. That God took on flesh, lived and died and lived again, conquering evil and death, and that the Spirit of God is with me now. That because of all this, I can hope that one day all things will be made new.

It's precisely because there was so much goodness in the evangelical communities I grew up in—in church, at home, in Christian schools—that this hypocrisy feels so shattering. There was goodness there, but something must have been missing, or flawed, in the way we understood virtue, and that's what I need to try to figure out.

I go to the library and check out a copy of *The Book of Virtues*. At home I scrutinize the pieces Bill Bennett chose to include. How did he select them? What did his choices show me about the way he understood virtue?

In the first of the ten sections, there are forty-three pieces. Six are unattributed, but of the thirty-seven others, only four are written by people of color—one from Clifton Johnson, and three of James Baldwin's retellings of folktales. Only five are written by women, and none of those five are by women of color. Bennett assumed his white, male voices could speak to and for all of America. The possibility that they might not didn't seem to enter his mind.

The pieces chosen reinforced mythic American ideals. Certainly anyone could succeed in America, Bennett's selections seemed to imply, if he cultivated self-discipline, responsibility, work, and perseverance; with these virtues, he could pull himself up by his bootstraps. Morality, after all, was an individual affair, not something that had to do with systems, which were of course neutral; and what was good was always plain to everyone. We were all on an even playing field, and the nebulous deity in whom we placed our faith, as well as the capitalist system in which we placed our faith, would always reward those who tried.

> *Bennett was looking for sources that reinforced what he already thought.*

It seems that in selecting the pieces to include in *The Book of Virtues*, Bennett was looking for sources that reinforced what he already thought. I began to understand that his treatment of virtue lacked a fundamental curiosity and basic awareness that ethical decision-making is complex; it lacked an understanding of the need to look outside the familiar for true insight. His vision of virtue was not panoramic and universal; it was myopic and self-referential. Could such a limited vision of virtue provide fertile soil for hypocrisy?

/3

A few nights ago, as my kids finished their dinner, I grabbed *The Book of Virtues* and read them the poem about Augustus, who refused his soup for five nights and then died. They loved it, dark ending and all. They asked for more, so I read them the poem about little Fred, who always went to bed quietly and obediently and said his prayers. After that, Owen, who is six, got up from the table and stood next to me, rereading both poems silently to himself.

I asked my friends online if they remembered having this book in their homes. "So many stories!" a few people said, happily. People remembered reading it alone or reading it with their parents in the evenings. None could remember a specific moral lesson they'd learned from the book, though a few suggested that stories from it probably generally reinforced other lessons their parents were teaching or modeling for them.

This makes sense, I think. Stories have the capacity to stir moral imagination, and research indicates that reading fiction can help build empathy. But the stories Bennett chose lack complicated moral questions. There are tales that may delight, as children are often delighted by the grim and the gory. There are tales that may teach—straightforward stories where good and evil are plainly defined. But there are few, if any, stories that are difficult enough to encourage critical thinking, few moral quandaries that are not easily explained. Even children know this to be a false picture of reality.

Stories have the capacity to stir moral imagination, and research indicates that reading fiction can help build empathy.

Children, like all human beings, live in an ethically complicated world. Stories that fail to reflect the complexity and ambiguity of real life fail to help children understand virtuous decision-making. Even in those cases where Bennett was drawn to a complex story, he selected a watered-down, cleaned-up version for his anthology, imposing queasy platitudes. Ethicist Miriam Schulman, reviewing *The Book of Virtues* on its publication, pointed this out:

> We need look no further than the Old Testament to find tales of unpunished betrayal and unrewarded piety that have, nonetheless, formed the basis of a great ethical tradition. Is it right, for example, that Jacob steals the blessing intended for his older brother, Esau? And yet Jacob is still the person God chooses to lead the tribe of Abraham. Grappling with morally problematic issues like this has provided grist for generations of ethical thinkers.

But Bennett does not trust the Bible to do its ethical work, selecting bowdlerized versions that make the stories conform to some preconceived notion of the proper message. In "The Long, Hard Way Through the Wilderness," Walter Russell Bowie's retelling of the Israelites' desert wanderings, Moses is an ever-patient leader, whose strongest utterance is "I am not able to take care of all these people alone. It is too much for me."

Compare that to the biblical outcry: "Wherefore hast thou afflicted thy servant? And wherefore have I not found favor in thy sight, that thou layest the burden of all this people upon me? Have I conceived all this people? Have I begotten them that thou shouldest say unto me, 'Carry them in thy bosom, as a nursing father beareth the sucking child . . .'?" Now that passage is moving. In it, a reader recognizes Moses as a human person and is inspired to ponder the whole question of discouragement and faith.

My children never asked for more from *The Book of Virtues* after that night at dinner. What they do ask for, night after night, are Bible stories. We cuddle in Owen's double bed under his light cotton comforter, me in the middle, the kids on either side so they can both see the pictures. We don't skip any of the stories, and I don't pretend to have all the answers to the questions they raise. Children know when a story has been cleaned up for their sake. They can also appreciate a story that can't be explained. The world doesn't always make explainable sense, so of course we have stories that confound and confuse.

Better than simplistic, moralistic tales attached to virtue are the unruly tales of the peasant Hebrews, which often lack easy answers or heroic characters. We may not be able to sum up these stories with quick ethical lessons or memorable proverbs, but in them we can Behold. We look outside of ourselves and our certainties. We behold comedy and tragedy and flawed characters: people who do wrong but still find success, and people who do right and are persecuted for it. There are no easy answers here, but there is something here about what it means to be human, about blood, about mystery, and about what it means to need rescue—and about a God who is always ready to save us.

Perhaps the moral failure of evangelical political leaders in 2016 shouldn't have been such a shock if *The Book of Virtues* is any indication of the larger problem. Such simplistic moralizing fails to practice the art of Beholding, of looking beyond oneself. It only ever shows us a sliver of what virtue could be, a simplified, whitewashed version of morality that isn't able to stand up against the ethical complexity of the real world.

> *There is something here about what it means to be human, about blood, about mystery, and about what it means to need rescue—and about a God who is always ready to save us.*

⚡

The word *virtue* comes from the Latin *vir*, for man. Its etymology is symbolic of much that is wrong with our current understanding of morality. For centuries goodness has been defined by those at the top of our historical hierarchies. They haven't always been wrong; but they have missed so much, and as a result, we live with—at best—an anemic understanding of virtue, an understanding of virtue that has gotten all tangled up with a political agenda, a set of "American values" that aren't Christian, sentimental ideas about the good old days, and a tendency to believe some voices more than others. In some cases, we live with a weaponized version of virtue that exists primarily to uphold the existing hierarchy.

Over the last couple of years, the moral failings of the so-called moral majority have been painfully obvious, and for those of us who grew up among them, this has been a kind of apocalypse.

We live with a weaponized version of virtue that exists primarily to uphold the existing hierarchy.

Originally, apocalypse didn't mean "the end of the world," as it is popularly understood now. It meant an uncovering, a disclosure of something that had been hidden, a revelation. So much has been uncovered: The hypocrisy of leaders who claimed to care about families and fidelity. The way the language of virtue has been co-opted to serve an agenda. The fact that the culture that taught me how to *be good* never really cared about my goodness. This uncovering has felt a bit like the end of the world for me. Or, at least, the end of *a* world.

But when a world ends, it's a chance to build a new one. Lament is the seedbed of hope, and now my post-apocalyptic landscape blooms.

This book is a record of both the lament and the new life. In it I grieve, and I get mad. I grieve the growing distance between me and my childhood communities of faith. I get angry at the ways some have used virtue-talk to try to control women and keep us in our place. I lament my pride and blindness, and I work to disentangle fear, certainty, patriarchy, consumerism, capitalism, and individualism from my understanding of virtue.

But the grief, the anger, and the lament have led me to a richer, more verdant faith, watered by voices I had never heard before and fed by perspectives I deeply needed; that's also part of this book. Reimagining virtue while listening to these new voices has restored my hope in the continued goodness of God in our fractured world. I am beginning to see virtue now as a tool for cultivating wisdom, not a weapon to wield against enemies; as wild, not tame; as embodied, not just written; as multifarious, not singular; as relationally negotiated, not legislated.

This isn't a book of final, definitive answers about virtue. It may not help "anchor our children and ourselves in our culture, our history, and our traditions"—in fact, I hope it may unmoor us from some of those traditions, and from a partial, whitewashed version of history, and leave us thrashing about in the deep for a while as we seek to find our footing again. And maybe we won't find our footing again. Maybe, instead, we will learn to swim.

CHAPTER 1

LAMENT

AT THE CLIFTON HERITAGE PARK ON NASSAU, WE ARE STANDING ON A CLIFF overlooking the blue waters of the Caribbean Sea. It's January, but hot. We are sturdy American tourists in baseball caps and backpacks, shading our eyes and gazing off in a dozen different directions. The cliff is edged with wispy Australian pines, non-native invasive plants that cause soil erosion, and a green chain-link fence, no longer upright.

Just yards away from us, behind the chain-link fence, stone steps built into the land lead down to the water. Some call them the slave steps, our tour guide tells us, and others call them the pirates' steps. Recent hurricane damage has made them inaccessible, but our guide waves in their direction as she teaches us about the history of slavery in the Bahamas. We stand on dusty ground covered more by pebbles than by grass or sand—white and gray, a little tired, a little parched, a little sun bleached. Off the cliffs, the water glints sapphire, and oil tankers anchored not far from shore bob like rusty tin cans cut in half and set afloat. In a little while we'll go snorkeling a half mile from here. We'll see a dozen kinds of fish, rays, and a coral reef, and we'll come out spotted with crude oil, wondering how much of it we may have ingested and whether the stains will come out of our swimsuits, horrified by what is happening to the natural beauty of this area.

I watch the undergraduate students I'm chaperoning. They are honors students at the Christian college where I teach, bright and inquisitive and sheltered and devout; most of them have not yet found any need in their lives for lament. Now they gaze at the screens of their iPhones, snapping photos. They stand shoulder to shoulder with the cedar statues also on this cliff, looking out to sea. Carved from the trunks of cedar trees planted by Ponce de León, these women lean toward the water; they have been watching the coast for decades. Their faces are black and their bodies dry gray wood. Faded blue scarves wrap their heads. One's hip juts to the south. One's shoulders hunch with grief. One wraps her arms around her chest, as if to hold her heart in place. Each is scarred with rough parallel lines sawn slanting down her sides, marks of the slave captain's whip.

"They are looking toward Africa," our tour guide tells us, "their homeland." Our tour guide is a stocky Bahamian grandmother in a beret and khaki pants. "But they are not sure which direction Africa is in, so you see they are all looking different ways.

Or maybe they are looking for their children. Families of slaves were often separated and taken to different islands."

I lift my own phone and photograph the cedar woman closest to me. She seems, more than anything else, to be looking toward the sky, as if she knows both her homeland and her children are gone and will not return, and she will not stop asking God why.

Women have a lot of painful questions for God, perhaps more than men have. At least that's what I have seen in art as I've traveled with undergraduates for the past few years, helping expose them to new ideas and cultures. These cedar trees remind me of a sculpture I saw two years ago outside the Memorial Hall of the Victims in Nanjing Massacre by Japanese Invaders. When the Japanese occupied Nanjing in 1937, they slaughtered more than three hundred thousand Chinese civilians and raped twenty thousand women. They raped children, the elderly, and nuns. Often soldiers would go door-to-door, searching for a girl to gang-rape. When they were finished, they would pierce her through the vagina with a bayonet or a stick of bamboo. Outside the memorial hall, a giant bronze woman holds her dead child loosely in hands falling to the ground. Her legs are heavy, weighted, her back beginning to arch, her eyes blank toward the sky, her mouth a silent O.

They remind me, too, of what I saw in Italy, Mary after Mary after Mary cradling the baby who would die.

⚘

At some point I stopped attending chapel. Three times a week, nearly two thousand gather on the university campus to sing together and to hear someone talk about God. Chapel isn't mandatory for either students or faculty—there are no attendance checkers—but it is expected that we all attend as regularly as we are able, and most do. But at some point I found I couldn't attend without crying. Maybe it was September 2014, and no one had mentioned the death of Michael Brown or the protests in Ferguson from stage. Or maybe it was September 2016, the week after Hurricane Matthew devastated the Bahamas, home to many students at our school, and everyone was singing, without a second thought, the contemporary worship song about resting in God's embrace "when oceans rise." Or maybe it was September 2018, after the shooting in San Bernardino, and the shooting in Cincinnati, and the shooting in Bakersfield, and the shootings in Wisconsin and Pennsylvania and Maryland. It could have been any month, any year; at some point I couldn't do it anymore.

The music didn't move me the way it used to—the thrumming bass lines or the snatches of cello. I felt disconnected and invisible as the relentlessly optimistic, victorious anthems played, as hands raised, eyes closed, and the Spirit moved, it seemed, in everyone but me. Did we have to be happy all the time? Was that what it meant to be good? The music of faith seemed all upbeat and major keys. What I needed was some acknowledgment of the shattered nature of things—some acknowledgment that lasted longer than a minor bridge or half a prayer before eliding into hope and glory. I probably wasn't alone, but no one else seemed sad.

For most of my life, I was the one with hands raised. From seventh grade on, you would have found me in the front row at youth group, standing as the Spirit moved me, singing with sincerity.

Nothing made me happier as a teenager than singing praise choruses in candlelit rooms after midnight. But in those songs, and in most of our gatherings, we drew from a limited emotional register when we approached God, a limited vocabulary; we avoided the book of Lamentations and the sad psalms and camped out in "Consider it pure joy whenever you face trials of any kind," and "Give thanks in everything." This worked out okay for me in my sheltered adolescent life, but in my early twenties, when I experienced my first heartbreak, I didn't know what to do with my very real grief. It wouldn't go away, and I didn't have words for it.

Eventually I turned to the Anglican tradition, finding in set liturgical prayers containers for the emotions I couldn't contain, forms I could use to hold my formless, shape-shifting grief. This helped. But over time I realized the Anglican tradition, too, had limitations when it came to acknowledging grief: while those Anglicans who pray the Daily Office do engage with all the psalms, many psalms of lament are omitted from the Sunday morning lectionary readings—the readings we hear most often.

In the last few years I've needed more space for grief. I think often of those cedar women on the coast, unwilling to give up their lament until they get a reply. When Michael Brown was shot and killed in Ferguson, his body left in the sun for hours before being carted away in the back of a Suburban, Black activists on Twitter taught me to see what was happening. With those eyes I saw Trayvon Martin, Eric Garner, Tamir Rice, Philando Castile, and so many others. Tamir Rice was twelve; Cleveland police mistook his toy gun for a real weapon. There are twelve-year-olds across the ocean mining the minerals that go into making iPhones like mine and working in the garment factories pulsing out the clothes my children and others wear. I'm caught in cycles of consumption, dependent on fossil fuels, and the earth's temperature is rising, species are dying, coastlines are eroding, hurricanes are intensifying. Puerto Rico went without power for months; Flint has gone without safe water for years. The Dakota Access Pipeline brought violence against Native American people and property yet again. Children escaped violence in Syria only to die at sea; children escaped violence in Honduras only to be torn from their families and placed in cells at our border. Inequality between the rich and the poor spiked. We elected a president who has a long history of seeing women as—in his words—*pieces of ass*.

And while all this news pummeled me, I watched the friends, writers, activists, reporters, and politicians I followed on Twitter express their grief and their opinions and their hopes. They didn't all respond to every story, and their emotions and solutions varied, but they responded. Meanwhile, the evangelical leaders I followed on Twitter kept tweeting about abortion and gay marriage. One week—near the beginning of September 2017—floods were ravaging Houston, Bangladesh, India, and Nepal. Charlottesville was recovering from white supremacists and Nazis marching through its streets the week prior. President Trump had just pardoned an openly racist sheriff and was beginning his attempts to repeal Deferred Action for Childhood Arrivals (DACA), an action that—if successful—would have significant and violent repercussions for immigrant families. I drank my coffee and scrolled through Twitter, absorbing the images of rising water in the streets of Houston, until I saw what white evangelical leaders were tweeting about that day:

their newly released "Nashville Statement," which they saw as a historic and courageous statement in support of traditional marriage. In that moment it became clear to me: my people were not grieving the same things I was grieving. Instead, they seemed to remain willfully blind to them.

I am trying to remain in community with my evangelical brothers and sisters, but it's hard. I'm not sure I can keep going to chapel until I know the people in the seats next to me believe these things are lamentable. I can't go to chapel again until we find some way to sing dirges together, to let sadness be a regular part of our common life.

⅓

I didn't grow up with the practice of lament. In the past few years, when grief has overwhelmed me, I haven't had any idea what to do with it. Frankly, emotions frighten me—I always prefer ideas and books—and so when my friend Kelley suggested I look at the ways the writers of Scripture practiced lament, it felt like the right way to begin. Trying to figure out what to do with my grief sent me to the library and to the Bible, and I wrestled there until I could begin to understand it.

Here's what I am beginning to understand: lament is the practice of mourning what is wrong in the world and calling on God to repair it. We lament the sins for which we are responsible, the sins for which we are only indirectly responsible, and, perhaps especially, the sins for which we are not remotely responsible. We lament the things that are broken, whether or not we broke them.

Lament, then, is part of repentance—of grieving personal sins and turning away from them. But it's also part of grieving the large-scale injustices for which we may be only indirectly complicit, and those losses that have no evident moral failure or culpability attached to them, but which result from living in a fractured world. In other words, lament is a practice that is appropriate whether I am repenting of the lustful thoughts I've been nurturing yet again, or whether I am grieving the death of Michael Brown and the structural injustices that have historically privileged white people in America, or whether I am mourning the death of a friend to cancer. Lament is a fitting response in any of these situations.

But becoming aware of my need for lament and figuring out how to define it hasn't made practicing it easy. Repenting of my sins doesn't come naturally to me because I am prideful and often willfully blind to my own sins. I don't want to change or be changed. Lamenting the larger infractions in our world doesn't come naturally to me either because I don't feel I need to take responsibility for them and because many of them don't directly affect my life. Most of the time I live comfortably cushioned against disease and poverty and hunger and violence. And when I'm sad, even for good reasons, I tend to activate my British genes and get very chin-up and stiff-upper-lip about everything. *Stop wallowing,* I say to myself. *Wallowing doesn't help anyone. It's not useful to lie in bed crying all day. Be stoic and resolute and uncomplaining and persevering; be good.*

Exactly because lament doesn't come naturally to me, I need the church to help me practice it. But for most of my life, the church has encouraged my natural tendency to avoid or repress negative emotions and to shrug off systemic injustices as out of my hands, not my responsibility. I learned in church to repent of my sins, but this practice was brief, and I could turn immediately to the truth about forgiveness and grace. Once or twice I was led in prayers repenting of vague national sins—repenting that our nation had "turned away from God," for example—but without any real acknowledgment of the sin inherent in the structures that shape our daily lives. And when I was sad or angry, mourning the natural losses of living in a broken world, my emotions were usually discredited by other Christians. Weeping may endure *for a night,* they'd say, italics in their voices, implication clear: allowing grief to continue is selfish. My sadness indicated a lack of faith or was labeled "complaining." I even heard lament identified as an Old Testament practice, one that was no longer valid in our postresurrection reality.

Why have we been so unwilling to practice lament?

Maybe we don't lament because we don't truly hope. We have given up believing that change—real, radical change—is possible, and so we have learned to be content with less, with injustice, with the status quo. We don't cry out because we think there's no point to it—there's no one listening, there's no one with the power to change what is lamentable, no one who cares enough to intervene. And so we quiet our desires and become stagnant rather than troubled. It's not the lamenters who are without faith; it's those who have given up lamenting.

> *It's not the lamenters who are without faith; it's those who have given up lamenting.*

Or maybe we are more comfortable with praise than with lament because we can't see that our world needs a radical reordering. Especially in the white, middle-class churches in the United States I've called home, it's true the systems generally work pretty well for us and for most of the people we know, who are also people like us.

Theologian Walter Brueggemann suggests our financial comfort shapes the way we approach God in worship. "The well-off do not expect their faith to begin in a cry, but rather, in a song. They do not expect or need intrusion, but they rejoice in stability [and the] durability of a world and social order that have been beneficial to them." The well-off are often able to take care of problems they encounter; they see themselves as masters of their own fates who only rarely need intervention from God. In contrast the poor and oppressed and those who live with suffering live "aware of the acute precariousness of their situation." They see themselves as "a dependent people crying out for a vision of survival and salvation."

At least in some ways, the poor have a clearer view of reality than the well-off do. Wealth blinds us to our own vulnerability and need for a saving God. Wealth blinds us to the realities in our world that need to be lamented because those realities so rarely touch our lives. Instead of seeking deliverance, we "are concerned with questions of proper management and joyous celebration."

When I think about the ways I've worshiped throughout my life, I think it's fair to say my worship has been characterized more by "questions of proper management and joyous celebration" than by a sense of my own need for deliverance. I know it's right to praise God, but I'm beginning to understand why praise is incomplete.

Without an appreciation of lament as a practice that forms me into the person God would have me be, I've been missing something vital to my spiritual health; I've stymied my own growth.

Maybe lament can connect us rather than further divide us.

When grief interrupts me, it gives me a chance to embrace vulnerability and to align myself with others who are familiar with suffering. Instead of trying to ignore or pray away my grief, what if I allow it to deepen my understanding of the suffering others have experienced? Maybe practicing lament can help me love my neighbors better; maybe I can let my grief lead me into solidarity with the suffering ones rather than letting it trap me in fear, defensiveness, and violence. Maybe lament can connect us rather than further divide us.

�

"This is the day that the Lord hath made. To do anything other than to choose to rejoice and be glad in it is rebellion against providence," a male pastor posted on social media in the week after we elected President Trump. After all I'd been learning about the practice of lament, I couldn't agree with him. I could not choose to rejoice and be glad in the election of Trump, just as I could not choose to rejoice and be glad in any of the failings I saw in my own life, in the church, or in our nation. My lament was not a rebellion against providence. It was a rebellion against the forces of evil in our world, the fractures that have not yet been repaired, the fractures that I am unable to repair. I wasn't rebelling against God, I was calling on God to be God, and I was lamenting the fact that while our salvation is complete, it is also incomplete, it is already and not yet, it is accomplished and in progress.

To choose lament as a response to the election of Donald Trump to the office of the presidency—or as a response to any of the problems I see in the world—does not imply that my hope has been placed in a political leader or some set of earthly circumstances rather than in God. I can place my hope in God but still grieve the election of an indecent, dishonorable man to the highest office of our land. I can place my hope in God and still mourn the systemic racism and the greedy capitalism and the fearful exclusivity that dominates the culture. To lament injustice is not to give up on God; in fact, it is to proclaim my continuing need for God's salvation.

Lament is holy complaint. When I was a child, I learned to "do everything without complaining," and I had to pay my parents a quarter anytime I said, "That's not fair!" As a parent, I understand the impulse to curb the whining and arguing with tactics like these, and I've definitely quoted that verse to my own kids a time or two. But I also think grumbling and complaining and crying out to God about the unfairness that does exist in the world are important aspects of prayer. That's part of the reason why I've made it my ambition never to tell my kids to stop crying.

This hasn't been easy: after all, children cry about the silliest things. My five-year-old son might cry because I cut his sandwich into rectangles instead of triangles. My eight-year-old daughter cried just yesterday because she doesn't have a room in our house she can use to create her own recording studio. They cry about things that seem inconsequential to me, but I don't ever want to imply to them that being good equals not crying. I don't want to say, "Stop crying—it's okay," when they are experiencing the sense that something in the world is not right. I want them to learn to be attentive to that sense. There are a lot of things in the world that are not right, and lamenting those things is the first step to changing them.

⅓

Tahlequah lamented the loss of her daughter for a thousand miles, off the coast of Seattle, Vancouver, and Victoria, British Columbia, swimming unceasingly through the same cold waters that had held her safe through seventeen months of pregnancy. An orca, Tahlequah pushed her calf, who had lived for less than an hour, through the Pacific Ocean for seventeen days before letting her go—an unprecedented show of mourning that drew international attention. Tahlequah's pod of killer whales is endangered; they are dependent on Chinook salmon for food, but Chinook salmon are also endangered, so food is scarce. Tahlequah's baby wasn't just her baby; it was her pod's hope for the future. Now scientists say the seventy-five killer whales in the Salish Sea have only five years to produce offspring if they hope to continue to exist. I can't help but think Tahlequah knows this, and her unparalleled tour of

There are a lot of things in the world that are not right, and lamenting those things is the first step to changing them.

grief was a cry for humans to notice the damage we have done to natural habitats.

Orcas gestate for seventeen months. Tahlequah mourned one day for every month she'd bonded with her calf. Perhaps this is coincidental, but I doubt it. Lament needs structure.

That isn't to say there is a right way to practice lament. There's no formula to follow. Grief doesn't come with a handbook. But when I went to the library to study lament, I learned all sorts of fascinating things about the biblical book of Lamentations. Among them: the author of the book of Lamentations, like Tahlequah, found a formal poetic structure useful in giving shape to grief.

Lamentations is a book of five poems that express the grief, anger, fear, and despair of survivors in the aftermath of the destruction of Jerusalem. In the poems, multiple poetic voices— some individual and some communal—call on God to see and to act, but God's voice is never heard. The narrative choice to allow the book to finish without resolution or a divine note of hope honors the suffering of the wounded; the unresolved poem reflects the unresolved nature of grief.

The poems are formally structured. The first four are acrostics: the first verse of each begins with the first letter of the Hebrew alphabet, the next verse begins with the second letter, and so on. The final poem is alphabetic: it contains twenty-two lines, the same number of lines as the number of consonants in the Hebrew alphabet. Why, asks Kathleen O'Connor, a professor of Hebrew, write "poetry of sorrow in alphabetical order"? She argues that the artistic choice signifies several important truths about grief: first, that it is vast. Grief goes from A to Z, and then it goes from A to Z again—and again and again. It seems infinite; it is more than what we have language for. And second, this artistic choice signifies that grief needs structure. "The alphabet gives both order and shape to suffering that is otherwise inherently chaotic, formless, and out of control. . . . It tries to force unspeakable pain into a container that is familiar and recognizable even as suffering eludes containment."

The acrostics vary in length. The first two are twenty-two verses of three lines each, one verse per letter. The third poem is three times as long—there are three verses per letter. The fourth is shorter than all of the others, with only two lines in each of its twenty-two verses. In this we see that grief comes in waves, and that the waves vary in intensity, and that perhaps sometimes we are too tired to lament as long as we once did. "The shortening poems and shrinking alphabetic forms imply exhaustion, increasing numbness, and the loosening of structures to sustain confidence in God and in the future."

Old Testament scholar Leslie Allen sees flickers of hope in the changed structure of the final poem, the alphabetic. Its brevity indicates the beginning of closure, he argues. The change in poetic style hints toward an ending of "total grief." Perhaps most interestingly, the meter changes. While the earlier poems used the limping meter of the dirge, with three long and two short beats per line, the final poem opts for a "regular three-plus-three meter, apart from a few lines. The change fits the fact that the all-too-human dirge, which had eyes only for past sorrow and none for God or for any hope for the future, has been scrapped in favor of the format of the lament psalm. The lament psalm is a prayer to God and envisions a potential of renewal and restoration."

Lament needs form. It will come in waves that cannot be entirely predicted. God will seem silent. The suffering must be honored. Relief, when it comes, may be minor, more exhausted than triumphant. And we must expect to be changed by our grief.

ß

In some ways the book you're holding is the result of my practice of lament. I grieve what I have lost in losing my confidence in contemporary American evangelicalism. I grieve what white evangelicals in America have done in capitulating to capitalist greed, in prizing our own comfort over our neighbors' safety, in remaining blind to the racism in our hearts and our country, in raping the earth. I lament the ways in which I and we have failed to practice our cherished virtues well. For me to lament these failures does not imply there are no virtues to be found among Christians. Sometimes we have let love lead us; sometimes we have let fear lead us. I'm lamenting the times in which fear won. And I am lamenting them because I still have hope we can change.

I could, in my despair, keep quiet, stay safe, and repress my feelings. I could assimilate fully back into the evangelicalism of my youth. Or I could, in my despair, try to burn it all down: to destroy my childhood faith because it wasn't perfect, because it wounded me and so many people. I don't want to do any of those things. I want to lament, hoping that in lament I find space for new, more expansive and constructive ways of understanding faith and virtue; believing that by God's grace something beautiful can still be born from my grief.

13

A few days after meeting the cedar women and swimming in the oily waters of the Caribbean, we toured the nearest diesel plant. Our trip focused on issues of small-island sustainability, and this was one stop among many to observe resource use around Nassau. After the presentation there was time for questions. Mark's hand shot up. "We went snorkeling earlier this week," he said, "and there was fuel in the water. Our tour guides told us used diesel fuel is stored in tankers in the ocean, but the tanks are leaking. How do you plan to address this problem?"

The man, dressed in a dark suit and shiny shoes, responded with ease. "The containers are old," he explained, "and they are shared by several companies. So they are breaking down, but the responsibility for that is shared. We are still negotiating how to handle this."

Oil is leaking into the coral reef. Several companies store oil here. The responsibility is shared, and so no one does anything.

Actually, someone has done something although I didn't learn this until several weeks later. Where we swam, there were large gray, concrete sculptures installed on the ocean floor. They were forgettable—not particularly beautiful, especially compared to the vibrant, moving fish around them. I thought they had been placed there to attract tourists to the area, but I was wrong.

Made by Jason deCaires Taylor, these massive art pieces were installed underwater in order to become a new coral reef, a new marine habitat for those sea creatures who have lost their homes. The sculptures provide places for sea creatures to hide, grow, and breed. The largest sculpture, called *Ocean Atlas*, is of a Bahamian girl, curled on her side, holding the weight of the ocean on her back.

She is like the bronze statue in Nanjing, the cedar women on the coast, even me crying at the back of the chapel auditorium because the world is not right. She is carrying the weight, and in her grief she is making space for something new to flourish.

"Weeping permits newness," writes Walter Brueggemann, and the lamenting women know this to be true. As we left that sculpture garden in Nassau, our guide pointed out something I'd missed. A rusty iron plaque chained to a large flat rock bore the place's name: *Genesis.*

"Genesis is where everything began," she said. "This is a place of new beginnings."

CHAPTER 2

KINDNESS

AS WE GATHERED FOR MORNING PRAYER ON THE LAST DAY OF OUR WRIT-
ers' residency on Whidbey Island, I filled my coffee mug and nestled
into the corner of a sofa, slipping off my shoes and tucking my feet
under me. Our leader, a prison chaplain, welcomed us. Pulling off
his cap, he rubbed his bald head from front to back to front, meditatively. He asked us to get into groups of two or three and pray
for each other, and I think he told us to ask the Spirit to give us "a
word" for our prayer partner, a word that would encourage, that
would guide the prayer, that would stay with us as we left the island
that day. My partner was a petite poet a decade younger than me,
with wide eyes and dyed hair. "Amy is kind," she prayed. Though I
sensed her sincerity, I wasn't sure how I felt about that word.

Actually, I knew exactly how I felt about it—my immediate reaction was distaste. I worked to maintain a neutral expression, though, and to remain open-minded. I held the prayer at arm's length, studying it, like a piece of art whose appeal remained elusive to me. It was a Thomas Kinkade painting where I wanted a Picasso—it was sentimental rather than strong. I wasn't sure I was kind. I wasn't sure I wanted to be kind. But it wasn't the first time I'd heard it.

I was twelve and awkward the summer I went to Camp Soaring Hawk, and I didn't want to be there. For the previous four summers, I'd been a camper at His Hill in Comfort, Texas; but when my family moved from San Antonio to Arkansas for my dad's job, it meant we were too far away to drive to Comfort in the summers. My parents found a comparable sort of Christian summer camp in nearby Missouri and convinced me to give it a try.

His Hill was home. There I'd learned to shoot a bow and arrow, ride a horse, paddle a canoe, and rappel down the side of a wooden tower. I knew that gentle Socks was the mare I wanted to ride. I knew the exact bend in the river where the counselors, on Friday, would jump out and ambush our canoes. I knew how to rappel backward, face first, and I was the only camper who'd been allowed to try it, whirling and spinning and leaping down the wall.

At His Hill, my faith felt real. At the end of my first or second summer there, around a campfire on the final night, hands sticky with watermelon, we were invited to share something we'd learned that week. Heart pounding, I joined the line to speak. I don't remember now what I said, only the feeling of that pounding inside of me.

We had counselors who came from around the world; I had a crush on a British counselor named James, and my favorite counselor, Katherine, was from New Zealand. They'd all been studying together at Bible college in England. Texas was foreign to them; we were all foreign to each other; and I had never felt so at home. Decades later if I smell heat concentrated in dust and live oak and mesquite, I feel instantly at peace.

Soaring Hawk was a disappointment, but looking back, I wonder how my parents and I could have expected it to be anything else. It wasn't His Hill. And I was twelve, coming out of a horrible year at a new school, quickly losing the physical confidence I'd had as a child. The other girls in my cabin talked about things I wasn't ready to talk about, about bodies and boys. There was no creek and no rappelling tower.

Near the end of the week, each cabin prepared a performance for the talent show—a song, dance, or skit. Our cabin dressed up like the Brady Bunch and sang the TV show's theme song. I was Cindy, the youngest, with hair in curly pigtails, and I felt cute and also like I did not belong to that blended family at all.

On the last night of camp, in a cabin ceremony, each camper received a plastic bead. Its color symbolized a character quality or virtue the counselors saw in the camper. When they gave me orange for kindness, I couldn't hide my disappointment. Orange was my least favorite color, and kindness felt like an insult rather than an affirmation. Nice was the last thing I wanted to be. I wanted to be brave or wise or funny. Instead of feeling named or honored, I felt flat, like a soda that had been left open too long.

Kindness was the bead that you gave to the girl you didn't

know, the girl who didn't cause any problems, the girl who didn't do anything memorable, the doormat who faded politely into the background as others hurried over her. Kindness was a virtue for women who were taught to be accommodating while men were taught to be strong and assertive. I had learned this at church, where virtues were often gendered; but I was not interested in being an accommodating woman. I imagined my counselors making their designations. "Amy? I don't know. She's so quiet. Let's see which bead is left after we do everyone else. We can always give her kindness."

So twice now, in gatherings twenty years apart, I had been named kind by people who'd bunked a week with me. I didn't know quite what to do with this; but I did know that however my counselors and my poet-friend meant it, the word had come to mean something completely different to me, something wilder and more expansive and dangerous and much more difficult than bland niceness.

Shortly after that writer's residency on Whidbey Island, I started reading *The Kindness of God* by Catholic theologian and philosopher Janet Soskice. In her examination of the etymology of the word *kindness*, Soskice helped me see it for the first time as a strong virtue rather than a weak one.

"In Middle English," she writes, "the words 'kind' and 'kin' were the same—to say that Christ is 'our kinde Lord' is not to say that Christ is tender and gentle, although that may be implied, but to say that he is kin—our kind. This fact, and not emotional disposition, is the rock which is our salvation." I paused after reading this sentence to try to take it in, to try to peel the sentimental layers off my definition of kindness and replace them with this fact: to be kind meant to be kin. The word unfolded in my mind. God's kindness meant precisely that God became my kin—Jesus, my brother—and this, Soskice said, was a foundational truth about who I was. Not only that, but for speakers of Middle English, *Lord* had a particular meaning—a lord was someone from the nobility, the upper social classes. To say "our kinde Lord" was to say the difference in social or economic status between peasants and nobility was also erased through Jesus the "Lord" being of the same "kinde" as *all*, landowners and peasants alike. Jesus erased divisions that privileged some people over others.

But what did that mean for the people around me? I was happy to be the sister of Christ but less than thrilled, frankly, to admit kinship with all humanity; that would make me related to that guy wearing too much cologne at the soccer game, the kid who hit my kid at recess, the woman flirting with my husband in the park, the racist troll I blocked on Twitter, the boss who fired me when he found out I was pregnant, the neighbor who did target practice in his backyard when I was trying to sleep. I would prefer not to call these people my siblings. I would prefer to distinguish myself from them, to say I'm not *that kind* of person—I'm not the kind of person who wears too much cologne, flirts with other people's spouses, stockpiles guns. But, in fact, I am exactly that kind: we are kin. If Soskice is right, then practicing kindness requires, at minimum, a willingness to see the image of God in, and to find a point of honest connection with, every person—even, and especially, those I dislike.

Maybe summer camp is the perfect place to practice this virtue. Counselors came from all over the world to His Hill. We didn't all share nationality, ethnicity, or bloodlines. Every summer, I was put in a cabin with a group of girls who were strangers to me, not kin. And whether we liked each other or not, for a week we learned to live together—to see God in each other, to share food from common bowls at our table in the dining hall, to follow each other's flashlights home through the mesquite trees after chapel. Of course, my bunkmates didn't become my family, but in learning to live with them, I began to learn to look outside of my biological family and community and find new points of connection—to see God in people who weren't always like me.

> *Practicing kindness requires, at minimum, a willingness to see the image of God in, and to find a point of honest connection with, every person— even, and especially, those I dislike.*

While kindness calls on me to see the image of God in all people, I don't think it asks me to treat all my human kin in exactly the same way—kindness doesn't require me to love the girls in my cabin at camp in the same way I love my siblings (or my parents or husband or children). Recognizing my kinship with all humans does not negate my particular connection with blood relatives or my husband. God gives us particular loves, and it is right for those relationships to be different. But our particular loves are also dangerous, because we humans can tend to let our good love for our own families blind us to the ways our actions might oppress or hurt those outside our families, those in our wider circle of *imago dei* kinship.

This danger has always been implicit in our practice of kindness. After reading Soskice I logged onto the *Oxford English Dictionary* website, looking for more about the relationship of kindness to kinship. According to the OED, in Old English *kyndnes* meant "nation," or, in legal documents, a right to a title or piece of land based on inheritance. Kindness was a way of maintaining social classes rather than a way of removing barriers between people. Kinship was exclusive, dependent on bloodlines, and kindness was an inheritance, the land you owned thanks to a father. In Old English the upper classes had more kindness—more land, more inheritance—than the lower. Virtue was attached to wealth and to those who were "like us." Kindness wasn't about recognizing the image of God in others but about maintaining one's own image or social status.

This hasn't changed much. I see the same sort of "kindness" practiced in the United States today. Around the same time I was putting together these etymologies, I read an article about the impact of receiving a financial inheritance (or, as the Old English would say, a *kyndnes*). In a widely reported study from the Heller Institute at Brandeis University, researchers Tatjana Meschede and Joanna Taylor looked at the influence of inheritance on Black and white college-educated families. When they began their research, they hoped to find that education leveled the playing field, as it were—that a college degree could be the solution to the wealth gap between Black and white families.

Instead, they found education made little difference at all. What did make a difference? Family inheritance; intergenerational transfer of wealth. Here's how they summed up their findings: "Among college-educated black families, about 13 percent get an inheritance of more than $10,000, as opposed to about 41 percent of white, college-educated families. And about 16 percent of those white families receive more than one such inheritance, versus 2 percent of black families."

The average amount is also drastically different: more than $150,000 for white family inheritances versus less than $40,000 for Black family inheritances. What this means, Taylor explains, is that "black families, even college-educated black families, rarely get a 'transformative asset,' a chunk of money that enables you to pay off student loans, purchase a house, or move to a better neighborhood to send your kids to a better school. For white families that's much more common."

That trickle-down across generations of white families has a real building effect.

"The thing about wealth is that it's sticky," says Meschede:

Once you have it, it really sticks with the family. It puts people onto a much better trajectory going forward. And the way wealth is distributed in this country, it replicates with each generation. When we think about wealth, often we think about our individual standing, but it's so strongly linked to what's happening in your family and in your networks. We think about education as the great equalizer when, clearly, it's not. It's much more complex than that. There's so much more needed in order to support the black community toward closing the racial wealth gap.

Until recently I had only rarely considered how the family money I've received has both cushioned and propelled me. I have tended to think my success, such as it is, is born of my hard work. But reading about Meschede and Taylor's study woke me up. The plain truth is I've had all kinds of advantages, including grandparents who paid for my private school tuition, my summer camp, my music classes, my first car, and some of my first international trips. A small inheritance after my grandmother died also allowed my husband and me to pay off our remaining college debt, and so I've been able to live most of my adult life debt-free. Of course, my grandparents themselves worked hard for the money they left me, but they—and their grandparents and *their* grandparents—worked within a system rigged in their favor. The wealth my grandparents shared with me is money that was accumulated within a structure that favored white people over indigenous people or Black people. But I don't think about this often: it's easy to remain blind to structural injustice when the injustice bends in your favor and when you're working hard for your success anyway.

My grandparents' (and parents') kindness and generosity toward me—right and proper ways of expressing particular love—took place within a culture warped by injustice. And while I can be grateful for what I've been given, I have to acknowledge that this matters.

For a long time in America, unkindness was written into our very laws and conventions. White Americans refused to recognize our kinship with indigenous people and slaves exactly because we wanted to preserve our own wealth. White men left their assets only to some of their children: the ones born of their white wives, not the ones born of their slaves. While of course we have always been kin, our bloodlines mixing and mingling from the very beginning, our customs and our laws for most of our nation's history ignored that truth, and so inheritances stayed divided by color lines. Even once we realize this history, it's easy to pretend that it's only history—that it doesn't affect our lives now. Torri, a woman I met when I began volunteering with a local political organizing group, has helped me realize how recent these cultural changes are, and how our racist history still shapes our contemporary reality.

Torri has been researching her family history for years, and this fall at a church event on reconciliation, she shared some of her findings. Because she knows the exact part of Kentucky where her grandparents and great-grandparents lived, she has been able to learn a lot. She knows, for example, that one of her ancestors fought for the North in the Civil War. But at some point in her research, she hit a wall. Her ancestors' names disappeared. Eventually she found them—she thinks—listed without names; based on the location and time period, she believes the next step in her family tree is in a list of "farm equipment." Right there, with shovels and spades, her ancestor is listed: "three-year-old girl." A piece of property. Part of someone else's inherited wealth.

Torri remembers her great-grandmother telling stories about her sister, who was a slave. "She had a good master though," Torri's great-grandmother would say, and Torri, even as a child, would look skeptical. "Her master always made sure there was enough food for them. He would leave it in the pig trough."

The county where Torri and I live is famous for a double lynching that took place in 1930; she is distantly related to one of the victims. It was this lynching that inspired the song "Strange Fruit," and it was as horrific as you might expect: two boys dragged through the bars of their prison cell by a mob and strung up in front of City Hall. There's a photo of the event that shows a crowd of white onlookers, one man pointing, another smiling.

The man who took that photo made it into a souvenir postcard. (Apparently during that time, people didn't think that was a strange thing to do.) Thousands of copies sold, and again, a white man profited economically from the suffering of Black men. His financial inheritance passed on to his children, while the Black families in our community passed down an inheritance of trauma.

The failure of white people to see the image of God in their Black and Native American brothers and sisters is the unkindness on which our nation was built. It's an unkindness that has been financially profitable for us, and because of that we have often remained conveniently blind to it.

Considering the truth about my kinship with all humans invites me to consider what it might mean for me to share my inheritance, to work to make reparations on a personal level even for things like slavery and lynchings, things I am not personally responsible for and can never ultimately make right.

Perhaps we can learn to be kind, to love our particular kin in ways that aren't unkind to outsiders—ways that don't desecrate the image of God in others, but that honor it—by looking at the way God loves Israel.

Israel is God's particular love, God's chosen nation. But there is nothing in God's love for Israel that hurts or oppresses those outside of Israel. Quite the opposite: Israel is blessed by God in order to be a blessing to the nations. Through Israel, God's *hesed*—the inheritance of loving-kindness that God has for God's children—becomes available to anyone who wants to receive it. God's vision is for a wildly inclusive family, where any outsider can become a son or daughter simply by choosing to accept his offer. "And as for the outsiders who now follow me," God says through the prophet Isaiah, "I'll bring them to my holy mountain and give them joy in my house of prayer. They'll be welcome to worship the same as the 'insiders'" (Isa. 56:6–8 THE MESSAGE). God says the outsiders will have an honored place in God's family and city, "even more honored than that of sons and daughters" (Isa. 56:4–5 THE MESSAGE). Kindness is a family inheritance but not one available only to blood relatives or dependent on being the "right kind" of person. God's particular kindness to Israel was also extended beyond

> *God's vision is for a wildly inclusive family, where any outsider can become a son or daughter simply by choosing to accept his offer.*

Israel, to outsiders like Rahab and Ruth, who were not only added to the family but also made integral parts of it.

Isaiah's vision of kindness, of an inheritance available to anyone who wants it, isn't just about a spiritual inheritance. Being a part of Israel meant being included in Israel's community life, and one practice prescribed for Israel was the practice of Jubilee. Every fifty years debts were to be forgiven and land was to be returned to its original owners, so any economic divides between the rich and the poor that had developed over the course of a generation would be erased rather than entrenched.

I wonder how I would have felt if I had known any of these things about kindness when I received that orange bead more than twenty years ago. How might I have felt if I had understood that kindness isn't weakness? Kindness has little to do with being blandly nice, being the right *kind* of person, someone who won't cause any trouble by asking inconvenient questions, someone who willingly accepts the status quo and fills her place in society without troubling the waters. Kindness is, instead, about seeing the image of God in everyone, outsiders and insiders, and learning to love our kin in ways that don't oppress others. Kindness sometimes means breaking boundaries of bloodlines to become family and being willing to have porous borders. Kindness may require the redistribution of

Kindness is, instead, about seeing the image of God in everyone, outsiders and insiders, and learning to love our kin in ways that don't oppress others.

wealth as a part of justice. To have this sort of kindness requires real strength.

Kindness, however, is not a virtue either of the two major US political parties seems to understand. After all, partisanship by definition draws boundary lines between who is on our side and who we are against. While the Right may claim kindness as a moral value, the recent movement of many conservatives toward the white nationalist movement is a true failure of kindness. Alt-right recruiters rely on an us-versus-them narrative to cultivate fear in those who already feel impoverished and disenfranchised. The immigrants are coming for "our" jobs, they say, and these immigrants want to destroy our country, our way of life.

The Left doesn't have a great track record when it comes to kindness, either; they may be willing to accept refugees, but they are often unwilling to listen to their neighbors who have less education, less money, or a different worldview. For some liberals, people who own guns and believe in a literal six-day creation of the world are deplorable, not kin.

While admitting the real differences between us, kindness asks us to remember our interdependence, to let our love for each other be love that allows for the flourishing of all people rather than propping up structures that privilege *us* over *them*.

🖐️

Every morning while I'm waiting for the coffee to steep in the French press and toasting bagels for sleepy children, I watch the sky lighten over the cornfields east of my house. In the winter there's little to see but the stars winking away; in spring, though, the robins and the barn swallows are back, the morning sky stacks layers of color over the farmland, and my kitchen fills with light that's warm and pink and gold. Until I was introduced to the work of Robin Wall Kimmerer, it never occurred to me that kindness might have something to do with the way I related to this scene.

Robin Wall Kimmerer, plant ecologist, writes about the way language shapes our understanding of kinship. Kimmerer mourns the loss of her ancestors' Potawatomi language, which white settlers tried to extinguish. Her grandfather spoke Potawatomi as a child, but when he was taken to Carlisle Indian School, he was forbidden to speak it. He and all the native children at the boarding school were only allowed to speak English. For Kimmerer, the loss of the language she should have inherited is not just personal; Potawatomi contains wisdom that humanity will lose if the language is lost entirely, truths not articulable in English. Composed primarily of verbs, it has words for states of being that have no English equivalents. "You hear a blue jay with a different verb than you hear an airplane, distinguishing that which possesses the quality of life from that which is merely an object. Birds, bugs, and berries are spoken of with the same respectful grammar as humans are, because we are all members of the same family."

Potawatomi is a language less interested in things (as English is, being mostly nouns) than in animacy. Potawatomi grammar gives dignity to all life forms. English, Kimmerer argues, does not. To make her point, she turns to pronouns. Using *it* to refer to plants and animals deprives them of their animacy; using *it* allows humans to feel free to exploit the natural world without recognizing our relationship to it.

Kimmerer wonders what might happen if we found a new expression that could be slipped into English as a replacement for *it* when we are talking about living things, and she suggests one: *ki*. In Potawatomi, *aakibmaadiziiwin* means "a being of the earth," and she constructs her pronoun from the first part of that word. Ki clucks in the henhouse; ki curls up by my feet and wags ki's tail; ki rises from the fog over the lake in early morning. For plural, she suggests *kin*. On the blueberry bushes, kin are ripening purple, and in the lake kin flash silver through the water. "Our words can be an antidote to human exceptionalism, to unthinking exploitation, an antidote to loneliness, an opening to kinship. If words can make the world, can these two little sounds call back the grammar of animacy that was scrubbed from the mouths of children at Carlisle?" she asks.

Ki is unlikely to enter regular English usage; and yet since I read about ki and kin, I've found my perspective shifting. Now, when I stand in my kitchen waiting for the water to boil, or the coffee to steep in the French press, I look out the glass door across the back fields, and the scene is transformed. Frost tips the grass; our cat, Luna, paws at the door; geese honk, gracefully heading south. Now, I see all of this as kin, animated by the same Spirit that animates me. If God created all of this *ex nihilo*—simply spoke kin into existence— then certainly words have power. The word I use for these creations matters. And if God created humans not out of nothing, but out of the clay which God had spoken into being, then surely that frost-sparkled grass is my sibling, too, born out of the dirt like I was.

———

Such a thought skirts the edges of what was allowed in the Christianity I grew up in. It comes too close to being something we feared as much as secularism: a New Age philosophy. But to be clear, I don't worship the grass or the geese. And I'm not idealizing them. The poet Tennyson saw "nature, red in tooth and claw," and I see that in my backyard as well as in my human neighbors. We are all spoken into existence by God; we are all fractured by human failure, prone to violence and competition.

We are all spoken into existence by God; we are all fractured by human failure, prone to violence and competition.

I'm not worshiping the natural world. I'm recognizing our kinship, our shared status as created beings who are at once in need of redemption and able to praise our Creator. Kimmerer has helped me see this, and now that she has, I see that it has been in Scripture all along: Scripture speaks to our kinship with all created beings. God makes covenants not just with humans but with "all living creatures," birds, farm animals, and wild animals (Gen. 9; Hos. 2). God calls the stars by name (Isa. 40:26) and has compassion for all that God has made (Ps. 145:9). And it is not only humans who need redemption: all creation groans, waiting for it (Rom. 8).

Kindness requires us to learn how to exist with all living creatures and to admit how much ecological trouble we humans have created. Cultural theorist Donna Haraway suggests we must reconfigure the way we relate to Earth and all its inhabitants. "The task," she writes, "is to make kin in lines of inventive connection as a practice of learning how to live and die well with each other."

———

We must "make oddkin," she says, aligning ourselves with those creatures outside of our direct genealogical and biogenetic families, finding unexpected collaborations and connections because we will "become-with each other or not at all." If we hope to have an inhabitable planet for our children as an inheritance, we must begin to think even more expansively about who is our kin.

⋌⃗Ƨ

As I write this, I'm teaching a class called Reimagining Virtue. In early October, when we're studying kindness, I take students on a walk through the woods. As we step down the soft forest path, we pass oak trees and other slender trees whose names I don't know; we navigate carefully around poison ivy and pause in surprise at a patch of friendly orange mushrooms, dozens of them.

"Don't eat them, Camryn," Heidi jokes, as Camryn kneels in the dirt.

"They look edible, that's all I'm saying," Camryn replies. They do look like chanterelles; but none of us knows enough to be sure.

"If mushrooms are our kin, though, should we even eat them?" someone asks, only sort of joking. We had just begun reading the work of Robin Wall Kimmerer.

"Well, that's the question, isn't it?" I say. I don't like to answer their questions right away. And anyway, I'm not sure I have a good answer yet. So, as usual, I throw the question to the whole class. "What do you think? What does kinship require of us?"

They are uncharacteristically quiet.

"Let's keep walking," I say. We follow a short path to a spot by the lake where rough wooden benches form a circle, and we sit scrunched together in the only shady patch. It's hotter than it should be in October. I pull out our text from Kimmerer and read portions aloud to them, pausing to ask questions and allow for discussion, and pausing, too, when Hannah finds a spider dangling next to her seat. After deliberation—is the spider our kin?—she decides to let the spider stay. Despite this resolution, we have trouble coming to any definite conclusions as to what it means to recognize our kinship with the created world, so I pivot the discussion a bit.

I ask them about their responses to the study that's just been released by the United Nations' scientific panel on climate change. Most of them don't know what I'm talking about; a few have a vague idea from a headline they saw on social media. I summarize the findings, as best as I understand them. We've experienced one degree (Celsius) of global warming from the preindustrial period to now, the study says, and once we surpass 1.5 degrees, we can expect some or all of these things to happen: thousands of species will go extinct, entire ecosystems will vanish, and 99 percent of the coral reefs will be dead. We'll have increased flooding; more malaria and dengue fever; decreased yields of maize, rice, and wheat; and some coastlands and islands will be totally underwater. The study suggests that if humans don't make dramatic and immediate changes, this could begin within the decade.

"So isn't it too late?" someone asks. "I mean, none of us make the laws or run the factories or control emissions standards or whatever. What does it matter what we do?"

Another student pushes back. We don't do the right thing

because it will give us the outcome we want; we do it because it's right.

"What is the right thing, though, for those of us who have little power over the larger systemic issues?" I ask. "And what does this have to do with kindness?"

A student mentions Wendell Berry; another tells a story about a trip he took, studying small-island sustainability in the Bahamas, and his conviction that we ought to seek to really know the places where we live. As they talk, I notice a mother and son—homeschoolers, I think—picking the last, late blackberries at the edge of the forest, not far from us, and I wonder if they can hear our conversation, and if so, what they think of it. Most older evangelicals I know dislike this kind of talk. When I bring up the environment, they speak dismissively of tree huggers; they praise entrepreneurs who can make money, regardless of the costs to the ecosystem; they assert our "dominion" over the earth; and they may even remind me that it's all "going to burn" someday anyway, regardless of what we do. Evangelicals have been quicker to associate care for the earth with New Age "religion" than with Christian responsibility. But perhaps there's been a generational shift. I decide to ask.

"How does this relate to God's call to Adam and Eve to exercise dominion?" I ask. They begin to answer, but then we realize our class time is over; we have to start walking back.

As we wend back through the forest, breaking up into smaller groups, conversations continue. The consensus seems to be that the human responsibility to "rule" the earth isn't license to "rape" the earth. Rather, we are to consider how our decisions can lead to flourishing for all species, not just our own. This, I think, answers the question about eating the mushrooms too; determining what we owe to each other means thinking about how our actions contribute to our species' mutual flourishing. Foraging for mushrooms is better—for me, and for the world—for the mushrooms' kin as well as for my own descendants—than grilling a steak over charcoal. Many of the choices we could make that would be good for the earth would be good for us too.

They might be difficult. They might require sacrifices. They might slow our economic growth. And when I consider our history with making choices for the good of the group rather than for the good of the individual, I'm not optimistic. We are not kind people; we remain willfully blind to our siblings when doing so will line our pockets. At least we did when it came to our Native American siblings, whose land we wanted; and our Black siblings, whose labor we wanted; and we remain blind to the humanity of our immigrant siblings, some of whose labor we would like but most of whose needs we would like to ignore; and we remain blind to our plant and animal siblings, whose wealth we want to exploit. I fear that, once again, we will refuse to acknowledge our kinship and stay focused on maintaining our own finances, our own inheritances. We will choose to ignore the fact that climate change affects the most vulnerable humans first, and hardest, and that it's already affecting them; we will once again care for ourselves instead of making oddkin, instead of caring for those outside our immediate biological families. I hope I'm wrong; my students, in their openness and curiosity, their deep conviction and willingness to learn, give me some reason to hope.

———

13

Perhaps it's not too strong to say that the future of life on earth depends on kindness. It depends on us waking up to kinships indigenous peoples could have taught us about, had we been listening, and reconfiguring the human exceptionalism that has characterized Western culture. And it depends on us finding inventive ways to connect beyond our biological and biogenetic families, admitting our inheritances are not really ours but ours to share. Theologically, our redemption is only possible through "our kinde Lord," God making oddkin with humans, becoming like us so we can become like God. When we let this truth take root in us, perhaps we will learn to find joy and purpose in every new kinship we discover: like children happy to be forging new friendships at summer camp, crowding onto rough wooden benches around the campfire, listening to the crickets and watching the stars.

CHAPTER 3

HOSPITALITY

A FEW YEARS AGO, WHEN MY KIDS WERE ABOUT FOUR AND SIX YEARS old, I began to have doubts about our determination to have just two children. When Jack and I had made the decision, two seemed perfect for us. We hoped to be able to travel or even live internationally with them, sooner rather than later—having another kid would slow us down. Plus, both of us had aspirations in careers that—though not particularly lucrative—were demanding. And I had not liked being pregnant. Sciatica had made walking difficult for months, and in my first pregnancy, after my water broke, I endured three full days of labor before my daughter was finally born. On top of that, I had realized I don't really enjoy infants; I prefer a kid who talks back to a kid who spits up.

Then (oh, the pregnant then!) I went to China for two weeks, and something about being away from the snuggles of my no-longer-baby babies left me thinking: maybe I did want another one. Mine were getting too big! For the first time, commercials on TV with teeny tiny babies left me feeling misty-eyed and empty-armed.

I wiped my eyes and began to interrogate the desire. Where was this coming from? Did I want cuddles? (Yes.) Did I want diapers? (Lord, no.) Did I want sleeplessness? (Ha.) Did I want Christmases? *Oh.*

I realized it was mostly about the Christmases.

I am the oldest of five children. My mother is the oldest of five children. I've always known Christmases loud and full, with too many places squeezed around the table and every seat in the car filled, the entire pew at church taken.

The more I thought about it, the more I realized I was afraid of quiet Christmases. I was afraid of the hypothetical future Christmas when both of my kids would be married and with their in-laws, and Jack and I would be bereft, cooking something un-festive like steak salads and eating in front of the TV. I wanted another child to shore up my chances, to guard against that possibility of some-day being alone.

Never mind that Jack and I love quiet and solitude, absolutely adore it, can easily spend days on end reading and writing and rarely seeing other people and be perfectly content. Never mind that we love steak salads and sitcoms. I am one of five. How can I be the mother of only two? How could I bear even the possibility of a quiet Christmas?

To put this all more bluntly, my sudden twinge of desire for a third child was a desire born of fear, not of love; and if it wasn't born of love, how could I believe it was a desire from God? But I also realized God was prompting me to pray about expanding our family in other ways, about opening hospitably to strangers, to those who weren't related to us by blood.

What if I let my fears of one day being alone connect me to those who were alone now? What if I remembered that God had always put the lonely into families in unexpected ways: that Moses was adopted by a princess, that Jesus was adopted by Joseph, that on the cross Jesus instructed his mother and his beloved disciple to be family to each other?

Maybe the desire of my heart wasn't for another child. But maybe there was a single friend who wanted an adoptive family—who wanted to live with us, or if not that, at least to have local people to list as her emergency contacts, people to watch TV with, people to talk to about which vacuum to buy or the best way to cook salmon, safety-net people, people for whom hanging out was a given. Maybe there was a widow or a widower. Maybe there was a child who would need us for now or forever. Maybe there was an international student who needed a family away from family. I at least needed to pray about that.

Adding a child to the family is exhausting: a newborn's incessant needs and utter dependence lead to sleepless nights and call for all kinds of sacrifice. Perhaps, I mused, I shouldn't expect hospitality to be free of those kinds of demands.

I wrote down all these thoughts and posted them online, asking, "What might the family of God look like, if all of us prayed about expanding our families in nontraditional ways as much as we prayed about whether or not to have another kid? I think it might just look like too many places squeezed around the table, and every seat in the car filled, the entire pew at church taken. It might just look like love."

I hit Post on my blog and changed nothing in my life.

13

Here is what I believed about welcome when I was a child. I understood that wombs were to welcome babies; abortion was wrong because of Psalm 139. God was knitting kids together in those wombs. I understood that cliques were wrong, and that my group of friends needed to be hospitable to new friends because James the brother of Jesus had said that believers in Christ must not show favoritism. I understood that church, especially, was supposed to be a welcoming place.

My earliest memories of church are happy ones. My parents were founding members of a small, nondenominational church in San Antonio where Dad was an elder and led the praise songs on Sunday mornings. I remember playing spies with my friends on the wooded church grounds; and Dad on acoustic guitar, leading the whole congregation in kids' songs with hand motions and words like "I've got the joy, joy, joy, joy, down in my heart"; and Miss Janie teaching the children's Sunday school, going straight through the Old Testament, not skipping the lovably gory stories of Ehud assassinating the fat king Eglon and Jael hammering a tent peg through the head of the evil general Sisera. I remember the gently rushing water of the Frio River, where I was baptized when

I was ten on an all-church weekend retreat. After I rose out of the water, buried with Christ in baptism, raised to walk in newness of life, I hopped on the water slide built into the riverbank and slid wildly back into the water. Church was a place where fitting in was always easy and engulfing.

I was about seven years old when I realized that being a part of the church meant being open to newcomers. I decided (probably at the urging of my mom) that since I belonged there so comfortably and wholly, I had a responsibility to greet those who were new and unsure of their own belonging. Instead of focusing on my desires, I had a responsibility to look out for others, particularly those who were visitors or struggling to fit in. That very Sunday a new family showed up, and my best friend, Sarah, and I made sure to include Mikhail, the little blonde girl our age, in our games. A few months later Sarah moved away, and I was so glad I had made friends with Mikhail. She would be my favorite playmate for the next several years. I had welcomed the stranger, as my faith taught me to do, and I had been blessed. Making new friends seemed as simple as that.

I had welcomed the stranger, as my faith taught me to do, and I had been blessed. Making new friends seemed as simple as that.

Of course we also understood hospitality to be about parties. To this day I love throwing somewhat elaborate parties, like my birthday party last June, in which dozens of people of all ages came over for grilled bratwurst and homemade Twinkies. We played lawn games and built a bonfire and watched lightning on the horizon; most of us slept in tents at the back of our two acres, then had chocolate-chip pancakes and lots of coffee the next morning. My love for hosting crowds of people comes directly from the Christmas parties my family had when I was a child in San Antonio. Several families would come over, and we would walk through our neighborhood with a couple of guitars, singing carols to the neighbors, who would sometimes bring us cookies and sometimes join us on the walk.

When we moved to Arkansas, I wanted to continue the caroling tradition, and so every Christmas I invited friends over to have cocoa and cookies and go singing through my neighborhood. These memories are complicated, though, by a sting of shame. One house on my street was home to a gay couple. They never came to the door when we sang. Every year we'd ring the bell and sing the first verse to "Silent Night" or some other carol, and then, when the house stayed quiet and shut, we'd switch songs. We'd sing "God Rest Ye Merry, Gentlemen," laughing to ourselves about the "merry gentlemen" who lived within, or we'd go into "Deck the Halls," singing just a bit louder when we got to "don we now our *gay* apparel." The men were different; I suppose we felt that gave us license to add mockery to our tidings of comfort and joy.

What a failure of love, to weaponize Christmas carols against our neighbors! Two decades later I still think of them every Christmas. I wonder if they refused to open the door to us because they'd been hurt by Christians before we showed up. They probably had good reasons to be wary when a group of evangelical teens came knocking in the midnineties; we proved their fears to be legitimate. The memory settles hard as iron in my chest each December.

And so my parties were not truly hospitable. I hosted friends, but we were never interested in welcoming those who were unlike us or whose presence might make demands on us or call us to change.

13

My understanding of hospitality expanded when I moved from being the welcoming one to the one in need of welcome: I became the stranger. At twenty-two I moved to a small town in a poor province in rural Southeast Asia. I didn't speak the local language. I couldn't identify half the foods on display in the market. I knew no one except my Canadian friend Lisa—she and I were both teaching English classes at the university. If it weren't for the warm welcome students and colleagues gave us, we literally might have had to subsist on instant noodles and pirated DVDs.

Sometimes I found myself at the mercy not just of my students and friends but of utter strangers. Near the end of my first year there, having learned a bit of the local language and grown comfortable getting around on my own, I planned a night of solo retreat at the coast, about fifteen kilometers from my home. Riding my electric motorbike away from the university campus, dusty gray streets soon gave way to rice fields, bright and young, lining the road, and as I picked up speed, the wind brought relief from unrelenting heat.

Another motorbike pulled up next to mine. The driver, like all women in the country where I lived, had dressed to protect her skin from the sun: long sleeves, long pants, a hat, and a scarf across her face. She pulled the scarf down, revealing a wide smile.

"Hello!" said the smiling woman.

"Hi," I replied, trying to hide my annoyance. I was retreating, for crying out loud. I was trying to be alone. But in that part of the country, many locals had never seen a foreigner, and they always wanted to talk with me.

"My name's Leigh!" she exclaimed. "You American?" I answered yes, hoping the conversation would end quickly. And after another line or two, it did.

"Oh! That my house," she said, slowing to turn and pointing to a small wooden house on a cement slab in a sea of rice plants and palm trees. "I invite you to my home!" she said.

I thanked her but waved goodbye.

Checking into my hotel, I asked the proprietors to plug in my electric motorbike so it would be fully charged for my drive home the next morning. Then I grabbed my books and journal and headed to the beach.

After a day and a night in quiet and prayer, I was ready to return to campus and finish the semester. But halfway home, my motorbike began to lose speed. Soon I was crawling along at no more than four kilometers per hour, and I realized the hotel proprietors had not, in fact, left my motorbike plugged in all night. They had probably wanted to save money on their electric bill. My motorbike was out of power.

I looked around. There was not a person in sight, just a haze of green, green heat and the buzz of mosquitoes. I was still nearly ten kilometers from town, and I was in trouble: even if another person came by eventually, it's not like they could bring me a gallon of gas. I didn't need gas; I needed an outlet.

And then I realized something: at the very moment my motorbike was dying, I was driving past Leigh's house. The woman who had introduced herself to me the day before lived right where I was, in the middle of this very rice field. I turned down the dirt path toward the cinder block home of the exuberant stranger.

Leigh was happy to see me and happy to let me plug into an outlet on the side of her house. Now that I saw her off of her motorbike, I realized she was pregnant, nearly full-term, and probably only a few years older than I was. Leigh invited me to sit down and pulled out a hairy coconut and a machete. Fascinated and a little scared, I watched as this petite pregnant woman split the coconut in half and poured its juice into two glasses. She offered me one and joined me at the table. With our limited knowledge of each other's languages, we floundered through an hour of conversation, sharing our lives and stories. She told me about attending university, marrying her high school "darling," and moving to his palm tree farm. He was often away on business, leaving her alone and pregnant. She wrote letters to her classmates who had married foreigners and moved to Australia and England; she missed them. I told her about the family I'd left behind in America, and about my job teaching English at the university. Thanks to her generosity, I eventually made my way home.

In the fourteen years since I ran out of power on a stretch of deserted rice field in Southeast Asia, I've often thought back to this moment as emblematic of the great hospitality consistently offered to me there. I was a stranger in desperate need; I was unable to demonstrate my trustworthiness, unable to prove I deserved help, and unable to offer compensation, yet I was warmly welcomed and cared for.

The way I was embraced when I was a stranger in Southeast Asia sparked in me a desire to extend the same kind of hospitality when I came back to the States. A couple of years after returning, my husband and I moved into a shared home with international students in Seattle's U District. For three years we lived in one bedroom in the house and rented out the other seven bedrooms to students from China, Taiwan, Korea, Indonesia, Japan, Nepal, and Cameroon.

I was unable to demonstrate my trustworthiness, unable to prove I deserved help, and unable to offer compensation, yet I was warmly welcomed and cared for.

With our housemates, we practiced intentional community. We shared cooking and cleaning responsibilities, ate dinner together five nights a week, and met once a week for prayer. On Friday nights we hosted a dinner and Bible study regularly attended by about thirty additional international students from the neighborhood. Around the same time, a community group at my church started reading Christine Pohl's *Making Room: Recovering Hospitality as a Christian Tradition.* From that book I learned that welcoming strangers had always been central to the identity of the people of God— for us, hospitality was to be not an anemic friendliness to newcomers at church or matching table settings and menus that met Martha Stewart's standards, but a vigorous and sacrificial virtue, a posture of emotional, physical, and spiritual openness to strangers.

So when the global refugee crisis intensified in the 2010s, I had already been thinking about hospitality for a while. But I didn't realize the extent to which my experiences had distanced me from the mainstream white evangelical understanding of the scriptural call to welcome. When Pew Research reported in 2018 that 51 percent of Americans believed the United States had a responsibility to welcome refugees but only 25 percent of white evangelicals agreed, my brain started spinning in confusion. In fact, of all groups polled by Pew, white evangelicals were the least likely to see any moral obligation to admit refugees. I tried to excuse it: maybe white evangelicals answered that way because the question was framed around national obligation, not Christian obligation. After all, there are legitimate disagreements on the right public policy choices related to citizenship, borders, and refugees. But for individuals and for communities of faith, there can be no denying our posture should be a posture of welcoming, caring, sacrificing, and sharing. Surely if Pew had asked if *Christians* had a responsibility to welcome refugees rather than asking if our *nation* had a responsibility, they would have answered differently. Wouldn't they?

I wanted to believe that. I wanted to believe they remember the stories that tell us who we are, the stories that Miss Janie had taught me in Sunday school: stories about Abraham welcoming guests who brought him a word from God, and Abraham's descendants, after being enslaved and then freed, being instructed to make hospitality fundamental to their way of life. "You know the heart of a sojourner, for you were sojourners in the land of Egypt," the law proclaimed (Ex. 23:9). Their experience of vulnerability was key to their understanding of hospitality. And while care for the stranger was recognized as a sacred duty based on shared humanity throughout the ancient Eastern world, for Israel it was explicitly legislated. Love for the stranger and love for the neighbor were—for God's people—commands on equal footing, with specific laws ensuring Israel wouldn't treat aliens unfairly. In fact, the command to care for the stranger is repeated thirty-six times in the Torah, more even than the command to love God. Jesus himself, once a child seeking refuge with his parents from the violent regime of King Herod, lived as a homeless man and asked his followers to see him in the faces of the hungry and thirsty and imprisoned.

But again and again I found Christians responding with fear, lack of scriptural knowledge, and a tight grip on their own political power. My Christian friends on Facebook posted about the need to defend our borders. A woman at a church retreat, after hearing me teach about hospitality, told me she'd been in church for forty years and never heard the verses I'd read about the responsibility God's people have to welcome strangers. And when I wrote an article for the alumni magazine at the Christian university where I was working, the word *refugee* was edited out. "Too political," the editor said.

Meanwhile, images of Syrian refugees in the news etched themselves onto the inside of my eyelids. That picture of a toddler washed up on a beach, the strip of belly showing between his navy shorts and red T-shirt, his knees and ankles together, gently crooked, his palms up, his mouth and nose pressed against the wet sand, the tide receding in the background. He had died trying to escape an almost certain death in Aleppo, drowned after his small boat deflated off the Greek island of Kos.

And the picture of a child the color of dust and blood strapped to a bright orange ambulance chair, flanked by filing cabinets and a red emergency kit. Dazed after surviving an air strike in Aleppo, he stared unseeing toward the camera. He had seen things he could never unsee. The trauma had settled into his skin with the dust, had moved into his DNA, to be passed on for generations.

As the violence in Syria escalated and parents desperate to save their children fled, the United States slammed the door in their faces. President Trump signed an executive order suspending entry to the US from Iraq, Iran, Libya, Somalia, Sudan, Syria, and Yemen. The order stopped the admission of refugees of the Syrian civil war indefinitely. Even those refugees who had been through extensive vetting, who were on their way here when the order was signed, were stopped and detained at airports.

The United States would not offer any permanent option for resettlement for those Syrians fleeing civil war. At the same time, conditions were escalating at the US–Mexico border. Gang violence had been growing in El Salvador, Honduras, and Guatemala since 2014, and the number of people seeking asylum in America from those countries spiked. In 2018, a new zero-tolerance policy at the border required that all caught entering the US—including those fleeing likely death—would be criminally charged and separated from their children.

In the first few weeks of this new policy, hundreds of parents and children were forcibly separated, including some children as young as eighteen months.

The American Academy of Pediatrics wrote to President Trump about the new zero-tolerance policy, noting it could cause lifelong trauma in children. Some evangelicals spoke out against it too. Matthew Soerens at World Relief led a campaign, and a coalition of Christian women used the hashtag #notwithoutmychild to advocate for refugees on social media.

It was in this context that Pew Research reported that only 25 percent of white evangelicals thought the United States had an obligation to help refugees. The same demographic of people who would fight ceaselessly to protect the lives of unborn babies felt no compunction to protect the lives of these mothers and children fleeing war.

↗3

Perhaps the failure to welcome refugees stems from a tendency to see only *some* biblical ideas as political. Some Christians can move easily from "You knit me together in my mother's womb" to a call for antiabortion legislation. But these same people might either ignore Old Testament verses about the duty to welcome the stranger or see them as calls to individual action, not national legislative action.

Or perhaps our failure to welcome refugees stems from the lack of kindness demonstrated in my junior high caroling parties. We sang for those who were like us and sang mockingly for those who weren't. We lack the ability to see those who are unlike us in ethnicity or sexual orientation or religious conviction as truly our kin, our kind. We have forgotten how to see the *imago dei* in all people, and our fear of whatever is unfamiliar overrides our ability to welcome.

To some extent this is a normal human response. Social psychology has shown that most people, particularly those from individualistic cultures, display "in-group bias," a tendency to believe and support members of your own group over those outside your group.

But for white evangelicals, perhaps the failure to see the image of God in the foreign bodies at our borders stems from something beyond in-group bias. Many of our ancestors spent decades as slave masters, refusing to see the image of God in their slaves and often using scripture to justify their ownership of other humans. Such action inflicts trauma on the slaveholder as well as the slave, and trauma imprints on our genes, our brand of trauma leaving us blind and hard of heart.

White Christians in America have been in power for too long. We have forgotten what it means to be in need, to be vulnerable, to be strangers. When I hear my friends in the church taking up arguments against welcoming refugees—arguments like *How can we be sure they are trustworthy? Maybe they're just pretending to be desperate. Won't they be a drain on our economy?*—I think about Leigh in the rice fields. She did not wonder if I was only pretending my motorbike was dead. She did not hesitate to share her resources with me. Granted, I wasn't asking to move in. But I also wasn't running for my life. She offered the hospitality that was appropriate to my need, and she offered it without reservation.

This is a virtue many people around the world understand better than most white American Christians do. Most of us have never been stranded on the side of a road. Most of us have never had to run for our lives. Maybe we have something to learn from people who have.

I decide to return to our flannel-board Sunday school stories to see what I can learn from Lydia.

13

On a missionary journey, the apostle Paul entered Philippi in Macedonia. He had journeyed there because of a dream in which a man from Macedonia stood begging him, "Come over to Macedonia and help us" (Acts 16:9 NRSV). But after several days in the city, no one—no man—had welcomed Paul and his fellow travelers. The text doesn't tell us where they stayed those first several days. Philippi had not yet been evangelized, and indeed it may not even have had a Jewish synagogue. So on the Sabbath, Paul and his companions went "outside the gate by the river" (v. 13 NRSV) where they supposed they would find a place of prayer. And they did. They found a regular religious community of women, including Lydia. Lydia, who hailed from Thyatira, was a "worshiper of God"—that is, a God-fearing Gentile who had not yet heard the gospel of Jesus—and a dealer in purple cloth. She and the other women welcomed Paul and listened to him preach. They were baptized, and then they prevailed upon Paul to come stay with them.

When I was growing up, whenever I heard the story of Lydia, she was described as a wealthy businesswoman who extended hospitality to Paul. But while I was investigating theological perspectives on hospitality, I found that the story is actually quite different. In

Arthur Sutherland's book *I Was a Stranger*, I learned that Lydia's name is an ethnicon, a name given to a slave that describes origin, nationality, and ethnicity. Lydia was a freed slave from the city of Lydia in the region of Thyatira who had likely been forced to migrate to Philippi upon receiving her freedom because freed slaves could only work in the same locale as their past owners if their work would not cause economic injury. Dying fabric was not the work of the upper classes: dye houses stank, as the process of dying wool involved large amounts of animal urine, and much of the work was done by hand, leaving the workers with stained hands and forearms, visible marks of a low social status.

Lydia and her household, then, were likely a group of immigrant women in a subsistence occupation. When Paul and his companions agreed to accept her hospitality, it was a case of foreigners welcoming foreigners, and it was a case of a lower-class woman "prevailing" upon Paul to stay with her. The word that's used—"she prevailed" (16:15)—signifies force. It indicates that Paul needed to be convinced, and it implies that Lydia was saying, "If this gospel you preach is real and you and I really are now brother and sister, co-heirs with Christ, then prove it by being willing to come stay at my home." Her persistent appeals pressed beyond the cultural norm of female hospitality—that a woman should only host those with whom she was familiar or that only a person of wealth could be a host. Christ had changed that: based on their shared union with Christ, Lydia had authority to greet, receive, and protect the stranger who, in Christ, was no longer a stranger.

> *Paul needed to be convinced.*

The story of Lydia shows us that hospitality is not grounded in the availability of physical possessions, but in being possessed by Christ. Hospitality can be offered from one stranger to another (who may find they are not strangers, after all, but kin); it can break convention, it can be uncomfortable and blessed, all based on the identity we have in Christ.

The way Lydia invited Paul to welcome her surely shaped Paul's practical theology. Several years after that encounter he wrote, "Seek to show hospitality," and "welcome one another as Christ has welcomed you" (Rom. 12:13; 15:7). The word he used that we translate "hospitality" is *philoxenia*, which comes from *phileo*, a word that describes familial love, and *xenos*, the word for stranger. Rather than *xenophobia*, Christians are to demonstrate *philoxenia*. We are to love strangers like our sisters and brothers. Over and over again, the writers of the New Testament call for Christians to demonstrate this stranger-love. "Show hospitality to one another without grumbling," the author of 1 Peter wrote (4:9), while the author of Hebrews reminded readers of Abraham's experience: "Do not neglect to show hospitality to strangers, for thereby some have entertained angels unawares" (Heb. 13:2).

Over and over again, the writers of the New Testament call for Christians to demonstrate this stranger-love.

If we never venture "outside the gate," if we stay safe and secure in our silos, free from fear in our cloistered communities, how will we meet Lydia? How will we ever know our own need?

13

I broke the news to Jack while we cleaned the kitchen one night. We would be welcoming a third child into our family.

But this child was twenty years old. And this was probably— okay, certainly—something I should have conferred with Jack about.

I'd met Greta when she interviewed for the honors program at the university where we worked, just a couple of months after my blog post about not having any more babies. I'd interviewed dozens of students that day, but later, in admissions meetings, fought for only two of them. Greta was one of the two. She was a petite girl with pale blonde hair and a tendency to turn red when she spoke. She'd performed moderately well in the interview, making a few unconventional observations that signaled strong critical thinking skills; and she seemed to have an ecumenical background, attending evangelical churches and Catholic school, which broadened her perspective in interesting ways. I thought she'd be a good addition to our program, but it was more than that. While I'm wary of using Holy-Spirit-talk, it felt a bit like the Spirit was asking me to see her.

When Greta enrolled, she was fresh off a summer stint with a missionary team. She began classes with a burst of evangelistic fervor, hungry to see revival come to our Christian campus. Several weeks in, we had coffee, and she confessed she hadn't found community as intense and spiritual as she had hoped. She was thinking about dropping out of school to return to missions. She asked me, over another coffee halfway through the year, if it was possible to live always with such passion, and at first I didn't know how to respond. "No," I said, after a moment. "I guess I don't think it's possible. Even if it is, I'm not sure it would be healthy." I told her about the dramatic movements in my own spiritual life and what I'd learned from quiet fallow periods.

I had Greta in class that first semester, and though she blushed whenever she spoke, she made coffee dates with professors every week and arrived with lists of serious questions. Over winter break I traveled with her honors cohort to Italy. On our bus ride after visiting Assisi, she sat with me and asked why we shouldn't all be monks and nuns. Few students seemed to be seeking truth as intently as she was.

I'm not sure what happened to her over the next year. Faith drained away like the color in her cheeks, anxiety set in, realizations came that come to everyone at some point, about the ways the people who love you most have failed you and have been wrong. And then she came to terms with her sexuality, admitting for the first time that she wasn't attracted to men, but to women. Her relationship with her parents deteriorated, and depression ensued.

And somewhere in there I said that if her parents were indeed going to stop supporting her financially, she could live with us.

It was not enough, when I looked at the problems in the world, all the people who needed homes and didn't have them. It was not enough, it was barely anything, but it was a small thing I could do. Greta moved in with us a year after the Syrian baby washed up on the coast. She moved in with us while children fleeing gang violence in Central America were separated from their parents at the US–Mexico border. She moved in with us while our lawmakers made it harder and harder for any asylum seeker to enter the

United States. In the face of all this, making Greta my third child was a tiny gesture toward a new definition of family, a new way of thinking about who exactly it is that I am to care about, to be responsible for.

It was a small thing, but it was not without risk. Greta's mother, a lawyer, sent me threatening e-mail messages. And we took Greta in during the same period that the board, administration, and faculty at our university were embroiled in fierce debate over an official statement on human sexuality. We were untenured faculty, and our willingness to support a gay student in this way sent a signal to people who might be defining our professional future—a signal that would certainly be noticed, and that would not work in our favor.

Greta lived with us for ten months. We cooked meals together, played board games, and watched Alfred Hitchcock movies. We talked about budgeting and meal planning and the poetry of Christian Wiman and our favorite albums of the year. Greta dropped out of school, got a job, and applied to transfer to a state university. She cautiously offered a bit of her heart to her first girl-friend; they broke up, and they got back together, and they broke up again. Slowly, she began to reconcile with her parents and work through her anxiety.

She only came to church with us once or twice. Again and again I had to confess to God how much I wanted to save her—to make everything right for her. Again and again God reminded me that saving people was God's job. My job was to open the doors of my home and my heart.

Greta moved out. She only needed a family for a while (though she still calls me her pseudo-mom). And when she moved out, my Twitter feed was still full of stories about parents and children being separated at our border, about refugees fleeing violence and only finding more violence. My small thing was a small thing. Still, it drew me a step closer to solidarity with the vulnerable, a step closer to understanding my identity as someone who knows what it is to be a stranger, cared for by God, and able to welcome other strangers.

Hospitality, after all, is not just about greeting visitors at church or hosting swell parties. It is a radical stance of faithfulness against fear, grounded in an awareness of human vulnerability. Many middle-class Americans—many of the people I went to college with, many of my friends—have forgotten how deeply vulnerable we actually are; we've forgotten that we live and breathe at the mercy of God and our neighbors. If we remember, though, won't our hearts be more open to the defenseless and marginalized? If we remember that we are strangers, we will welcome strangers.

God told the Israelites in Leviticus that the land they'd been given was God's. They were to reside in it as strangers and aliens. Peter echoed this thought in his letter to Christians, calling us "foreigners and exiles" in the world. Hospitality is at the heart of the Christian identity; it was my mother who taught me this when I was seven. It was my father who modeled hospitality to children in church, leading us in songs that made us feel like we belonged there. Hospitality is an openness of heart, an openness of home, a stranger welcoming a stranger to a space where we can slide wildly into the water of life together, where each person can be more fully herself, can flourish, can come closer to a home that will endure, a kingdom that cannot be shaken.

Greta wasn't with us for Christmas, but she was for New Year's Eve. My sister and her husband, driving cross-country, stopped to spend the holiday with us and brought their friend Tam. Katie, Elliott, Tam, Greta, Jack, and I welcomed the new year together that night. We made good food, and we played good music, and every seat in the room was full—and it looked a lot like love.

CHAPTER 4

PURITY

FIVE TEENAGERS ON STAGE, UNDER A CROSS. LANKY OR SOFT, PERFECT or pocked, all thrum with nervous kinetic energy that gives off an almost audible hum, *zimmmm*, like an electric current in the air or, we sometimes think, like the Holy Spirit. They are beautiful. On command, one by one, each takes a mouthful of water, swishes, then spits into a cup that is passed down the line. At the end, the man with the microphone offers the cup to the audience. "Who wants to take a drink of this?" We laugh. No way. That's gross.

Or one man on stage, under a spotlight, holding a perfect red rose. As he talks, he plucks a petal, another, another, another. They float to the floor; he preaches, paces, and forgets the object in favor of the lesson, bruising the petals black beneath his Converse tennis shoes.

Or a group of girls, fourteen years old. This one loves horses. This one plays trombone in the school band. This one still reads *Anne of Green Gables* every year. They follow instructions. They paste two paper hearts together and wait for the glue to dry, pushing at the damp spots where the paper has grown dark and soft. They pull the hearts apart, but now the papers stick together in places. Rather than a pure blue heart and a pure green heart, the girls now have hearts that are blue-and-green and holey.

13

In the nineties, for evangelicals, the word *purity* took on a singular meaning. If a pastor or a youth pastor preached about staying pure, you could be sure he was not speaking broadly about holiness or philosophically about Kierkegaard's "Purity of Heart Is to Will One Thing." No, he was talking about sex—to be specific, about not having it unless you were married and married to a member of the opposite sex. Purity defined this way, or used as a vague synonym for *virginity*, was everywhere in the nineties; it was the evangelical response to the sexual revolution. Elisabeth Elliot's *Passion and Purity*, published in 1984, told the story of her courtship and marriage to Jim, and encouraged young Christians to stay "pure" while waiting on God's timing for romance. In 1992 we got DC Talk's anthem "I Don't Want It (Your Sex for Now)"; shortly after that, Joshua Harris published *I Kissed Dating Goodbye*, and Rebecca St. James sang "Wait for Me," an abstinence theme song that could be purchased along with the companion journal, study guide, or the book, *Wait for Me: Rediscovering the Joy of Purity in Romance*. A generation of young people signed purity pledges and wore purity rings.

There are many questions to ask about the origins and motivations of this purity culture, but for me, one of the most interesting is this: Why was *purity* the word chosen? Scripture barely connects the word *purity* to sex. The vast majority of references to purity in the Bible are in the Old Testament and have to do with precious metals used in temple construction, with incense, or with rituals for staying clean and presenting yourself holy before God. Some of those rituals were related to sex—but not all or even most. Throughout the Bible the word is sometimes used as a synonym for *righteousness* and in calls to holiness. Only one verse in Scripture connects purity to the relationship between men and women—and it's not about sexual relationships. First Timothy 5:1–2 says, "Treat younger men as brothers, older women as mothers, and younger women as sisters, with absolute purity" (NIV). Here pure relationships appear to be ones that are familial in tenor.

If defining purity as "sexual abstinence until marriage" isn't exactly a scriptural idea, it also isn't a logical one. Consider the most basic definition of purity: to be unmixed. One can see how abstinence is a kind of purity, by that definition; but if unmixed-ness is the kind of purity we are to seek, then all sex is impure, even sex within marriage. Sex is exactly mixed-ness.

Maybe I'm being too literal. But words matter, and precise definitions matter. Of all the virtues I've set out to reimagine, purity feels the most fraught with danger and misuse. I've seen too many people hurt by purity culture; sometimes it has made me want to give up on the idea of purity altogether. But I don't think I can. Understanding the true meaning of purity was, for me, a three-part process. First, I needed to understand why and how the language of purity had so often hurt people rather than leading them to fulfilling, God-honoring relationships. Then I needed to ask: If *purity* is the wrong word to use to talk about sex, what are the right words? And, finally, I had to try to figure out what purity in the Bible is actually about, if it's not about sex, and how I can practice it well.

∕3

Tina Schermer Sellers, a therapist and professor of sexuality and medical family therapy, wrote in *Sex, God, and the Conservative Church* that over her decades of practicing and teaching, she observed a marked generational difference in her clients and students based on whether they grew up in the church during the height of the purity culture. Those who had grown up in conservative Christian homes in the 1990s and early 2000s exhibited "profound levels of sexual shame and dysfunction" in comparison to those who grew up in the 1960s to 1980s. In exploring the reasons for this shift, she found that purity language was one culprit.

In the early 1990s, the no-sex-before-marriage discourse was expanded to include the idea that Christians must remain "sexually pure" before marriage, which many Christian youth understood to mean refraining from any expression of sexual desire: no masturbation, kissing, longing, touching, fantasizing, and so on. The vagueness of words such as *purity* and *sexual abstinence* used in teaching and in the pledges these youth were asked to sign left young people confused and overly self-restrictive in the development of their erotic selves. What does "purity" look like anyway? And by implication, what are the "impurities" that a person is supposed to avoid? Are my romantic and sexual desires bad? Perverted? What does "sexual abstinence" refer to?

Having pledged themselves to such a vaguely worded promise, many teens found themselves plagued by shame about any erotic feelings or experiences. As a teen in the nineties, I was too skeptical of authority to really buy into what purity culture was selling, so I managed to exist on the margins of it without being too damaged. But from friends, my siblings' friends, and my students, I've heard story after story that illustrates Sellers's researched conclusion that connecting the idea of purity to teenage sexual identity can be profoundly harmful. One warm spring day during final exam week, two students shared such stories with me.

Hannah was twenty-one and a month away from her marriage. In the cover letter to her final portfolio of work in my creative nonfiction class, she told me she was including an essay that no one else had read. She had written and revised it in private because of its content.

I pictured Hannah—light freckles, uncertain smile—as I opened the document and began to read. The new piece was titled "Painfully Pure." In it she described her first visit to the gynecologist. She had waited until a couple of months before her wedding for her first exam—ever. She found it painful and disconcerting, and the experience triggered her many anxieties about sex.

> Suddenly I felt utterly unprepared. In one night I was supposed to transform from a perfectly pure virgin into a competent, capable wife without any preparation or instruction. I had had years of learning what I shouldn't do but no one to tell me what I should. My first visit to the gynecologist only confirmed the fact that my body wasn't ready—physically or emotionally—to make this transition. Sex went from taboo to terrifying. . . . Even after more extensive premarital counseling and conversations with other engaged and married women, I still find myself placing my worth and value in my virginity or, once I'm married, my ability to perform sexually.

Hannah went on to describe her shifting theological convictions about purity: "I'm discovering that the problem with Purity Culture is that it ignores the miraculous healing of Christ and places the problem of purification on imperfect people."

A thoughtful, self-aware, sincere student with good friends around her, Hannah was able to process her shame and anxiety about her upcoming honeymoon in exceptionally mature ways. But even she was entering marriage weighted down with all kinds of guilt and false expectations (issues that, months after her wedding, she tells me she and her husband are still trying to work through).

Purity culture teaches kids to be absolutely abstinent so that their marriages will not be haunted by the specters of past loves. Purity culture intends—at its best—to keep any adolescent mistakes from hampering the health of a marriage. But, instead, it often sends kids like Hannah into adulthood burdened with other baggage: shame, anxiety, pressure, and even terror. Some take years to recover from the damaging messages they internalized about sex. Some have sought escape through self-harm and even suicide. Some of my friends, the kind who didn't kiss until their wedding day, have divorced because they were unable to connect sexually.

An hour after I read Hannah's essay, Rachel came by to drop off her portfolio. She stayed to chat.

"I was rejected from grad school," she said. We discussed other possibilities in front of her—some good local jobs, a couple of other grad programs—and then she said, "Also, I could be pregnant."

I didn't try to hide my shock. Normally I take student confessions pretty calmly, without registering my own emotional response, but this was legitimately startling, as Rachel had also told me in the last month that she was pretty sure she was gay.

"I don't even know why I told you that," she said, smiling that uncontrollable nervous smile of the very emotional or the very anxious. "I didn't mean to."

"I guess you want to talk about it," I said.

"I guess I do," she said, and went to close the door so we wouldn't be overheard.

It had been her first time having sex with a guy, and the condom broke. She thought she was safe anyway because of the timing. But now she was two days late, and she was starting to freak out.

What had made her decide to have sex? She hadn't been drunk, and it wasn't just a hookup—she'd known the guy for a while. He attended a school in a nearby city. They'd met through mutual friends and talked a lot. She'd decided to have sex with him because she was trying to figure out if she was gay. It hadn't helped, really—she said she felt sort of detached from the experience, but in general, she often felt disconnected from her body. She'd grown up so afraid of having sexual feelings, she told me, that she had managed to mostly turn them all off.

Purity culture had left Rachel ill-equipped to know her own heart, mind, or body.

She had experimented with women first. She'd had a threesome with a lesbian couple. It had made things emotionally complicated for them as friends (which somehow had caught her by surprise); their relationships took six months to recover. But neither experience had made her sexual identity clear to her. We talked for a while about attraction, connection, and how to make wise decisions; but I drove home from campus that day fuming.

Purity culture had left Rachel ill-equipped to know her own heart, mind, or body. To try to stay "pure," she shut it all off, and now she can't figure out how to turn it on again in a healthy way. She struggles to know herself. She is flailing. Meanwhile, Hannah will enter her young marriage with significant hurdles to overcome: little to no understanding of her own sexual desires and needs, and lots of shame and fear.

/3

What made purity culture so wounding? Turns out it was as much its metaphor as its message.

At the recommendation of a friend who was a survivor of both purity culture and sexual abuse within the family, I stopped by the university library to check out psychologist Richard Beck's *Unclean: Meditations on Purity, Hospitality, and Mortality*. My friend had found it helpful in understanding internalized shame, and I was intrigued by the combination of words in the subtitle. Beck introduced me to the psychology of disgust and explained why the purity metaphor was so powerful.

When you are sick, you usually get well, and when you are in the dark, you know that the sun will probably rise soon enough. When you see yourself as impure, though, it's psychologically harder to imagine becoming pure again.

We have many metaphors at hand when it comes to talking about sin, Beck pointed out. We can talk about being dirty, perishing, being in debt or enslaved, lost, sick, in the dark, orphaned, blind, dead, or asleep, to name a few. These metaphors are all biblical, and each has its own emphasis, carries its own unique emotional and psychological weight. When you fall asleep you can easily imagine being woken up again. When you are sick, you usually get well, and when you are in the dark, you know that the sun will probably rise soon enough. When you see yourself as impure, though, it's psychologically harder to imagine becoming pure again. And that's why using the purity metaphor for sexual sin is so dangerous.

Psychologically we believe that purity once lost is lost forever.

—

Imagine that you came to your picnic table to find a cockroach doing laps in your glass of lemonade. Would you simply remove the cockroach and drink up? Most people wouldn't. In his laboratory, Paul Rozin has found that even if that contaminated lemonade is then filtered through the kind of filter used to purify tap water—or even filtered, boiled, and then refiltered—most people still refuse to drink it. His research demonstrates that "judgments of contamination play by their own rules," rules that aren't logical. Even if, rationally, we can understand that the lemonade is clean and perfectly safe to drink, we cannot overcome the emotional response.

When it comes to purity, our judgments are also conditioned by what researchers call dose insensitivity and negativity dominance. Dose insensitivity is the idea that it only takes a single drop of contaminant to effectively ruin something, and negativity dominance teaches that the unclean is more powerful than the clean. If a drop of urine is added to a liter of soda, most people will not drink that soda. A single drop of something unclean is more powerful than a much larger quantity of something clean. For teenagers, this response might translate into a belief that the smallest sexual purity infraction can make them utterly gross and beyond fixing. Once that drop of urine is in the Coke, it's ruined beyond repair.

Although all sins might, generally speaking, be considered purity violations, few sins are "specifically regulated by purity metaphors," Beck writes, in the way that sexual sin has been in American evangelicalism. Tying sex to purity in this way also connects it to the psychology of disgust. Disgust is a normal human response to those things that are bodily offensive. We spit out spoiled milk. If we step barefooted into dog poop, we wipe it off, grimacing at the odor, and wash with plenty of soap. Disgust at these "boundary violations" is a normal biological response, but what disgusts us also has some "degree of plasticity" dependent on culture. Babies respond with disgust to very few things: they put whatever they can grasp into their tiny mouths and suck meditatively. Disgust, then, is both innate and culturally learned.

Disgust monitors the boundaries of our bodies to keep us safe, clean, and pure. Purity culture taught us to respond with disgust to sexual contact that breached our bodies' boundaries. The skit in which several teenagers all spit into the same cup, and then the audience was asked to drink it—this skit was designed to trigger a disgust response, and to connect sexual activity with disgust so that teenagers would refrain from having sex. And while it is right to cultivate disgust for those things the Bible teaches are disgusting, and to cultivate a "taste" for those things the Bible teaches us are good, the Bible teaches us that *sex* is *good* and a gift from God. Triggering a disgust reaction for teenage sex does not help humans live a holy sexual life, because linking disgust to teenage sex also links it to all kinds of sex.

Triggering disgust for sexual activity by using the purity metaphor teaches people that sex is gross; it teaches that the smallest sexual infraction makes them disgusting, that nothing can overcome their disgustingness, and that nothing can erase it. Psychologically, the way we respond to purity violations can lead us to believe that our sexual sins are more powerful than Jesus and that our shame is intractable. Even if we can see logically that these things are not true, we struggle psychologically to believe them.

———

Because this is how humans respond to the purity metaphor—and because the Bible itself doesn't use the word *purity* in regard to sex—I find no reason to try to reimagine purity as a virtue that has anything to do with sex.

But we do need to talk about sex. I'm not sure exactly how. I'm not certain which words are best. I'm still figuring it out. My kids are young, but so far here's what I've tried to do with them. I've always used anatomically correct language when we talk about bodies, and I've tried to make body-talk a natural part of conversation, without shame or embarrassment. I've answered questions honestly and directly. I've drawn my kids' attention to advertisements or song lyrics that paint false pictures of romance and sex and taught them to think critically about what they see and hear.

When Rosie, at six, came home from school singing Taylor Swift's "Blank Space," which had been playing over the speakers in the gym during PE, it was a chance to discuss what Taylor means when she says, "Boys only want love if it's torture." We got to talk a little bit about how boys and girls both want to find real love, and what real love looks like. I suggested that it doesn't look like falling for a pretty face and making a purposeful "mistake," and that it's not always about kissing in the rain—though sometimes it is. Later, when we were listening to "Stay Stay Stay," she asked, "Mom, what are 'self-indulgent takers'?" and we were able to discuss how to choose friends (and eventually boyfriends). You look for people who aren't selfish, who are generous and giving, and you try to be that kind of friend yourself.

I've also taught them that their bodies are their own: that no one can touch their bodies without their permission. I've taught them that *no* means *no*—so, for example, if I'm tickling them, and they say stop, I stop immediately. Their language about their bodies and their desires matters and should be taken seriously even when we're playing. I respect their boundaries and hope this will lead them to demonstrate and to expect the same kind of respect when it comes to boyfriends or girlfriends in the future.

This kind of talk about agency and consent isn't enough, though. It's important, but on its own, it's reductive. Basing a sexual ethic solely on consent would leave us pretending that sex is something we understand and can control, something rational, some exchange of goods. Sex is about more than agency. Longing can overthrow life. Sex is unpredictable and powerful—and so is marriage, which in some mysterious way, the Bible tells us, images the relationship between Christ and the church. To really talk about making good sexual decisions, we'll need more than just agency: we'll need words like *fidelity* and *attachment* and *covenant*, as well as *vulnerability*, *risk*, *respect*, and, of course, *pleasure*. After all, the most extended and straightforward discussion of sex in the Bible comes in the form of an erotic love poem that celebrates as *good* parts of God's creation longing, desire, mutual pleasure, and the body. This, it seems to me, must be foundational to any discussion of a "virtuous" sex life.

From there we can go on to talk about how the decisions we make with our bodies can demonstrate love for God and for our neighbors. Such conclusions are best worked out in individual conversations, where context and personality and life experiences and culture can be taken into account. What I would say to a teenager would be different from what I'd say to a woman in her twenties, or her forties—but the principles would be the same. Your body is good. Your desire for sex is not shameful. God asks you to make sexual choices that affirm the dignity and value of every person. God asks you to keep your promises. The Bible teaches that there is something mysterious and weighty that happens when bodies come together, and that the enduring commitment of two people to each other in marriage is a beautiful thing that, at its best, can teach us something about the way Christ loves us. Instead of talking about purity, I would begin there: with love.

So purity is not a virtue that is about sex. Using the language of purity to talk about sexual ethics has been more damaging than helpful, and we can find better ways to talk about good sex. But now I'm left wondering what *purity* does mean if it's not a synonym for *abstinence* or *virginity*. I think about the other contexts in which we usually hear the word *pure* in daily life.

A twelve-pack of Nestlé Pure Life bottled water costs $2.48 at Walmart. Of course, it's not actually pure water—that is, it's not pure H_2O—it's purified water. Drinking pure water could kill you. All the water we normally drink—from taps, from bottles, from the garden hose—contains impurities, salts, and sugars, which make it slightly hypertonic. If we drank pure water, which is hypotonic, our cells would start absorbing water, swelling, and bursting, leading to possible brain damage, coma, and even death.

Impurity makes it possible for me to drink water. Impurity also makes it possible for water to crystallize, which makes it possible for me to wake up this morning to a landscape transformed and quieted by a thick blanket of snow. Pure H_2O won't crystallize until temperatures dip down to negative 40 degrees Fahrenheit. But add a protein or some kind of particulate matter, and ice can form at 27 degrees. Soot or bacteria can form a nucleus, a kind of backbone that the water molecule structure needs to form snow. So "pure as the driven snow" should be rephrased. The snow we love to see out our windows in winter is impure, reliant on impurity, and beautiful because of it. Without the dirt at the heart of each molecule, we would rarely be able to see the beauty.

A desire for purity within a group sometimes results in painful division. Church splits and new denominations often have their roots in attempts to create a more morally or theologically pure body. The Puritans—who are not named for their relationship to sex, but for their relationship to the church—sought to purify the new Protestant church of any vestiges of Catholicism, and to keep church membership pure, so that it comprised exactly and only the body of the elect. And all kinds of fundamentalisms—religious, political, on any end of a spectrum—require this expulsive mechanism to maintain purity. Whether it's churches refusing to ally with gay Christians or the Women's March refusing to ally with pro-life feminists, the purity requirement cuts off the potential for fruitful cooperation.

Other calls for purity throughout history have, not to put too fine a point on it, been calls for death. Attempts to maintain a pure race, ethnic group, or genetic code have meant ending the lives or the reproductive capabilities of those judged to be adding impurity to the mix. The state "must set race in the center of all life. It must take care to keep it pure," Adolf Hitler wrote in *Mein Kampf*. Margaret Sanger, the woman who popularized the term *birth control* and founded the organization that would become Planned Parenthood, believed in compulsory segregation or sterilization for those she regarded as unfit. And when Pol Pot wanted to transform Cambodia into a socialist agrarian republic of Khmer nationals, his government sought to "purify the populace" by systematically killing ethnic and religious minorities, among others.

Donald Trump's attempt to build a border wall between Mexico and the United States is also about purity, and his language about immigrants has been critiqued as pre-genocidal, particularly his use of the verb *infest* to describe those coming to the United States. Before the Holocaust, Nazis also talked about "infestations" of "Jewish vermin"; similarly, the Hutu of Rwanda called the Tutsi "cockroaches." The Trump administration's decision to house detained children in cages is another way of dehumanizing immigrants, signaling that they are dirty animals, that they must be kept out of our pure nation, which must be bordered by a secure wall.

Thinking about purity in all of these contexts leaves me wondering if purity is actually a virtue at all. After all, impurity—mixed-ness—is necessary for life to exist, for babies to be created, for water to be drinkable, for snowballs to be packed by mittened hands in a Midwestern midwinter. And historically, calls for purity have often led to death and destruction.

But my confusion about how—or whether—to value purity is nothing new. In fact, faithful followers of God have often disagreed with each other on how to pursue purity—and on what things are worth sacrificing in its pursuit.

In the Old Testament, the books of Ezra and Nehemiah chronicle the restoration of postexilic Israel to their home and their temple, and the building of a wall around Jerusalem. God's people were in a precarious position. Between 987 and 597 B.C., the Babylonians had destroyed the southern half of Israel, including Jerusalem and the temple. But when the Persians conquered the Babylonians, the Persians sent the exiled Jews home to rebuild their temple and their city. The Persians were happy for the Israelites to restore their laws, customs, and traditions, as long as Israel could be a tax-paying colony and a buffer against Egypt.

This was all good for the Israelites, of course; the precarious bit was that in this supportive environment, Israel might easily lose its unique identity. The Persian Empire had placed Jewish leaders Ezra and Nehemiah in charge of the restoration, and they were serious about building a wall and reinstating the laws of the Torah. Among those laws was an eternal edict against intermarriage between Israelites and Moabites.

To preserve Israel's ethnic identity, and as part of returning to the laws of the Torah, Ezra and Nehemiah demanded an immediate end to all Israelite marriages with foreign women. In fact, they went further than that. They sent away all the foreign wives and children born of foreign wives. They broke up families in the name of ethnic purity and obedience to the Deuteronomic law. And in some sense, one can't fault them for this—they were being obedient to what was written, and they were in a vulnerable position; maintaining a distinct identity was important to their survival.

But the book of Ruth, which was written in the same period

as Ezra and Nehemiah were at work, challenges the claim that foreign wives ought to be rejected and indicates something about the nature of God. The story went like this: fleeing famine, Naomi and Elimelech settled with their sons in Moab. Both sons married, and then both sons and their father died. Naomi decided to return to Bethlehem, and her daughter-in-law Ruth decided to go with her. "Where you go I will go," she said. "Your people shall be my people, and your God my God" (Ruth 1:16). Once settled in Bethlehem, with Naomi's help, Ruth married "a kinsman on her husband's side" (2:1 NRSV), the noble Boaz, both skillfully using and flouting the law so that she could be incorporated into Israel. Their son Obed became the grandfather of David, Israel's greatest king.

Throughout this story the audience is repeatedly reminded that Ruth is a Moabite—"the young Moabite woman, who came back with Naomi from the country of Moab" (Ruth 2:6). And this Moabite—one who, according to Deuteronomy, ought not be allowed to marry into the family of Israel—became the great-grandmother of Israel's ideal king and, by extension, Jesus' forebear. The gently subversive tale of Ruth invited postexilic Israelites to ask what would have happened to Israel's history, as it were, if Boaz had divorced his Moabite wife and abandoned their son, as Ezra and Nehemiah instructed. It invited them to care for outsiders even as they sought to remain pure and obedient, and to question whether ethnic purity was the most essential characteristic of the people of God.

Purity, the story of Ruth suggests, has less to do with keeping yourself separate from the wrong kind of people and more to do with being engulfed in the love of God, a love that invites everyone in. It has more to do with *where* you are than with *who* you are. Ruth was in the right place when she was following God; that was more essential to her identity than her ethnicity was.

This fits with how social anthropologist Mary Douglas thought about purity. In her groundbreaking book *Purity and Danger*, published in 1966, Douglas analyzes the concepts of pollution, ritual purity, and taboo in different societies and eras. She argues that dirt only becomes dirt when it's out of place. Dirt on the forest floor isn't dirty, but dirt on your kitchen floor is. Hair on the head of your beloved is beautiful; hair in your soup is disgusting. Your saliva in your mouth isn't gross, but when those teenagers on stage spit into the cup, suddenly their saliva became gross. To be impure is to be in the wrong place.

Purity is about things being in their right places.

This insight might actually be the most helpful thing I've found when it comes to understanding how to practice purity: purity is about things being in their right places.

Instead of asking "How can I be pure?" and answering by pointing to a list of rules for appropriate sexual relationships, perhaps I begin to practice the virtue of purity by asking where I belong—where I fit in the world, what my right place is within it—and by accepting that my place is wherever Jesus is.

Where I belong is in this new kingdom that Jesus has brought to earth, a kingdom characterized by love rather than by fear of contamination.

Jesus was not afraid of contamination. He crossed one boundary after another in the name of love. He ate in the wrong places with the wrong people. He healed on the Sabbath. He touched the untouchables—the ritually unclean, the leper, the corpse. At his death the veil to the temple tore from top to bottom; now the holy place is the right place for anyone, not just for the few. Because of Christ, our categories are breaking down: "There is no longer Jew or Greek, there is no longer slave or free, there is no longer male and female" (Gal. 3:28 NRSV). Now, when we eat, we can be sure that "all things indeed are pure" (Rom. 14:20 KJV). We don't have to worry about the purity of the food, Paul wrote; all we need to consider is whether the way we eat or drink demonstrates love for our brothers and sisters.

When we love, our normal disgust triggers turn off. Or, as the poet William Butler Yeats wrote, "Love has pitched his mansion in the place of excrement." We change diapers and we catch vomit in our hands and we eat the slightly slimy leftover crusts of peanut butter and jelly sandwiches from our kids' plates. We make love and open to the mouth of another, let our tongues tangle. We ingest the body and the blood of Jesus, drinking from a common cup. Jesus, I think, if given the cup of spit from the teenagers in the skit, would drink it down and give his body in return.

Because in Jesus there is no negativity dominance. His love and purity are so strong that any impurity they encounter is immediately made beautiful. To be pure, to be in the right place, requires only this: to be with Jesus.

Definitions and boundaries and ordered systems still exist, but they no longer separate us from one another—they no longer need incite violent attempts to maintain purity.

In one of Jesus' last recorded prayers, he asked that his followers would be characterized by unity. Why unity and not purity? Perhaps it wasn't that Christ valued unity over purity, but that for him there was no conflict between the two. Jesus could take on the sins of every person and yet remain pure: he was stronger

I'll tell them that to be pure is to be in the right place. And the right place is wherever Jesus is.

than any impurities. His was not a purity by exclusion but a purity by inclusion. In asking for unity for his followers, he was asking that the many would become one in him and thus also become pure.

If I want to teach my children about purity, here's what I won't say. I will not tell them they might become impure if they start to experiment with sex. Instead, I'll tell them that to be pure is to be in the right place. And the right place is wherever Jesus is. His purity is so strong you never have to worry that something you bring to that place can sully it or make you disgusting or change who you are. The purity you have in being united with Christ is not something you can lose.

Purity means embracing your unity with Christ and, in that unity, becoming free to open yourself fearlessly to others in ways that are safe and healthy and truly loving—in ways that draw others into fellowship with Christ too.

Blessed are the pure in heart, Jesus said, for they shall see God. But such purity is not something to achieve through careful rule following. It is something to receive as the gift of God to you in Christ, and it is something that can never be lost.

We are, after all, pure as the driven snow: soot at the heart, washed in baptism, and made lovely.

CHAPTER 5

MODESTY

MY DAUGHTER IS NOW NINE, AND THIS MORNING WE HAD A TALK ABOUT the importance of dressing modestly. She came into the living room wearing boot-cut jeans, a loose white T-shirt with a sequined wolf head on the front, and a gray hoodie—all hand-me-downs from her older best friend. As she was slipping her homework into her backpack, she overheard a discussion Jack and I were having about his work wardrobe.

"I need new clothes!" she interrupted. "I only have, like, three pairs of jeans. And I feel like I wear basically the same thing every day," she said, gesturing to her outfit. We talked for a minute about how it's okay to wear jeans several times before putting them in the laundry and about how she has several pairs of leggings and sweatpants too.

"I think it's okay to wear basically the same thing every day. If you wore something new and different every day, that might not be modest," I told her. "If you had a lot of clothes, and you were showing off your wealth and your wardrobe by wearing new things to school all the time, that would be immodest." She nodded. She had known all along she didn't really need anything; she just wanted to get in on the shopping.

The desire to consume is strong. Maybe that's human; maybe it's exacerbated by modern American culture. Regardless, for us to buy our daughter more clothes would be wrong. We live in a rural area where most of the kids at school qualify for the free or reduced price lunch program. Spending our little disposable income on clothes that will be outgrown before the year ends would be unwise, and it would also be inappropriate to our situation: immodest.

That's not, of course, how I heard modest clothing described in my own childhood or adolescence, and it's not the most common way of using the word now, either. The word *modesty* is mostly used in reference to how much of a woman's body is covered by clothing, how much skin is showing. (And yes, this word is used almost exclusively in relation to women's bodies, not men's.) But modesty, at least as it's considered in the Bible, has little to do with how much skin is showing. When modesty is extolled as a virtue in the Scriptures, it's defined by a refusal to flaunt one's wealth or power. To be modest, Rosie doesn't need to start measuring the inches between the top of her knees and the hem of her skirt.

She has an innate sense of what kind of clothing makes her feel comfortable in her body, and I want her to continue to trust that. But she might need help with true modesty. She might need help learning to identify her wealth and power, and to use them for the good of her neighbors rather than thoughtlessly flaunting them. I need help with that too.

13

When an underground newspaper on our campus (claiming to be, in contrast to the official student newspaper, a needed "conservative voice") printed an article about the importance of modest clothing, I started hearing stories from students. One woman, working at the front desk of our student athletics center, told me she had been asked not to wear shorts to work because a male faculty member had reported being "distracted" by her legs. Another told me about the first time she felt ashamed of her body: when she was instructed by a youth group leader to wear a T-shirt over her modest tankini while floating the Kickapoo River. A third told me about a male faculty member whose syllabus included a dress code for women: they couldn't wear yoga pants or leggings to his class. There were no rules for the men.

These women weren't angry that their rights were being taken away: they were wounded. People they looked up to acted as if the female body was dangerous and shameful and ought to be hidden, and they weren't sure how to respond.

For the last few decades, modesty has been one of the biggest planks in the platform of evangelical purity culture. In youth groups and private schools, adolescent boys and girls are often separated for "the talk," in which boys hear about avoiding pornography and girls hear about the ways in which our bodies are, by their very existence, pornographic. Girls learn that boys cannot look at us without thinking about us naked and imagining doing things to or with us, and so keeping our brothers "pure" is our responsibility. We need to avoid short skirts and shorts, bikinis, and spaghetti straps. Before leaving home, we ought to do modesty calisthenics: bend forward and backward in front of a mirror to see how much cleavage or thigh is revealed; and then reach for the sky to make sure no strip of stomach shows. If we love our brothers, we will protect them by covering our bodies. And if they can't control themselves, the fault is at least partly ours; we have "caused them to stumble." This is what I'll refer to in this chapter as the standard "modesty doctrine" I grew up with: the idea that women are called to dress in a particular way so our bodies will not cause men to lust after us or to mistreat us.

This is . . . the standard "modesty doctrine" I grew up with: the idea that women are called to dress in a particular way so our bodies will not cause men to lust after us or to mistreat us.

Some of the problems with the way modesty was taught and practiced as a part of purity culture, and in evangelicalism broadly, are almost too obvious to name, but just for fun, let's name a couple of them. First, modesty was taught with a focus on outward appearance rather than character and behavior. Second, this interpretation of modesty conflated cultural norms and standards with eternal truth. By failing to discuss the importance of culture and context, we missed an opportunity to practice decentering our own experiences of the world and to practice understanding a moral issue through someone else's lens. How much more instructive might modesty lessons have been if we had read and discussed Elisabeth Elliot's description of life with the Huaorani (whom she calls the Aucas), who were "unhampered by clothing (or by washing, sewing, mending, or ironing) and the caprices of fashion (with the vanity, jealousy, covetousness, and discontent which fashion fosters)." Our modesty talk was a missed opportunity to practice thinking deeply, interculturally, and theologically.

The way we discussed our motivations for modesty was also a problem. The woman's inspiration for being modest was always double-edged: on the one hand, it was about loving our brothers in Christ. Our motivation was to be helpful to them in their own struggles with lust. On the other hand, we were told that ultimately "modest is hottest," and that while men might want to date women who dressed immodestly, they wouldn't want to marry them. The reasonings we were offered, then, were not just about loving our brothers but also about controlling them and getting what we wanted from them. We were encouraged to decide what to wear based on what effect we wanted to have on men: dress modestly, snag a husband.

While we young evangelical women tried to cultivate secret power over men through what we revealed or refused to reveal of our bodies, men often had literal control over what we wore. Fathers could approve daughters' outfits. Clothing was chosen with the male gaze in mind. Modesty was about power, whether it was about men having power over women's bodies or women using their bodies to gain power over men. This is a major problem! It is virtuous and loving to act with your neighbors' best interests in mind—but is it really virtuous to seek to control your neighbor?

There are deeply troubling implications about the nature of both men and women in this kind of modesty doctrine. Women learn to see their bodies as innately problematic. Women may also absorb the message that only men—not women—have active sex drives, and when women find themselves turned on by a shirtless guy at the pool, they may feel deep shame. And men? The modesty doctrine teaches women to see men as less human, as having less power over their own impulses than women do. If men are so weak that the sight of a bra strap peeking out removes their ability to control their thoughts or actions, then they must not have free will as women do or the ability to practice self-control.

The modesty doctrine taught us to be afraid of our bodies instead of recognizing them as good creations, gifts of God, and sources of knowledge.

The modesty doctrine taught us to be afraid of our bodies instead of recognizing them as good creations, gifts of God, and sources of knowledge.

༭

Though I've heard many horror stories about the way modesty teachings negatively affected my friends (and students), the truth is, I don't have any horror stories of my own. Modesty talk didn't dominate my adolescence. My mom and I may have disagreed now and then about what was appropriate for me to wear, but I never felt like the needs of men or boys were controlling my options. I understood that the choices I made in dressing could be a kindness to my brothers and (whether it was fair and right or not) could shape my reputation, and both of these things seemed helpful for me to know.

The effects of modesty culture on me were subtler. The modesty doctrine taught me to have low standards for men; when my college boyfriend confessed with fear and trembling that he looked at pornography, I shrugged. As far as I knew, all men did, so it was no surprise. Modesty doctrine instilled in me other false beliefs about what "all men" were like with regard to sexuality—that their desires were constant and insatiable, for example—which was not helpful to me as a woman in actual relationship with an individual man who did not always conform to those stereotypes. Further, it encouraged me to be judgmental of other women based on their clothing choices and to be prideful about my own.

The underlying assumptions of the modesty mind-set bled into my life in ways unrelated to my clothing choices too. It was an easy, natural mental move from "I should cover up my body to protect men" to "I should cover up my talents and gifts to protect men." When I began to believe I could care for my brothers by hiding my body, I also began to believe I could care for them by hiding my mind or my personality, which could be threatening. I learned to quiet my talents, to mute them, to use my gifts only in ways that would not intimidate men. Modesty, it seemed, demanded I ought not expose myself in any way: not my body, not my feelings, not my talents, not my anger, not my intellect. This was a way to protect myself (from rape, from hurt, from making men feel insecure or from turning them off); it was ultimately about defining and understanding myself principally in relation to men, about keeping my power hidden for their benefit, or for my own self-preservation.

Modesty encouraged me to hide rather than to learn how to use and develop my gifts. I hid my powerful body for the sake of others; I also hid my powerful mind and talents, letting them stay dormant—or even stagnant. It was the modest, womanly thing to do.

♫

Perhaps some reader has followed my argument but believes—despite the negative repercussions—that a modesty doctrine is still relevant, that women still ought always to dress a certain way out of concern for their brothers' well-being.

Perhaps this reader is right; and perhaps there is a way to talk about what clothing is culturally appropriate and fitting for men and women without prioritizing the needs of men, implicating the bodies of women, or turning our relationships with each other into relationships based on control rather than love.

But even if there is, I don't believe that such practice is what the writers of the Bible had in mind when they used the word *modesty*. Modesty, like purity, is a virtue we have defined as primarily about sex and primarily about women. But just as purity in the Bible is really not about sex, modesty in the Bible is only tangentially related to how much skin is showing.

𝄐

Two passages are commonly used to support the modesty doctrine I grew up with.

Women are often encouraged to choose clothing that will not be a "stumbling block" to men. This phrase comes from Romans 14, where Paul wrote to his readers telling them "never to put a stumbling block or hindrance in the way of a brother" (v. 13).

Romans 14 is a chapter about food and about the varying beliefs in the church regarding what was permissible to eat. Some Jewish converts to the Christian faith still followed Jewish dietary laws and kept the Sabbath; other converts believed they could eat anything, and they considered all days to be alike. Paul said the weaker brother is the one who does not yet understand that "nothing is unclean in itself" (v. 14). He asked the one who is stronger in faith to avoid quarreling over such matters and to avoid judging those who are weak.

Romans 14 is not about modesty, but the language of the "stumbling block" and the "weaker brother" were appropriated to the modesty conversation. Reading modesty into this chapter, though, is an inappropriate interpretive move. Let me explain why. Let's use Paul's argument in this chapter to analyze another (somewhat) contentious practice: drinking alcohol. Some Christians believe every believer should totally abstain from drinking alcohol. Other Christians see no problem with moderate drinking. By Paul's argument, the weaker brother is the abstainer, the one who is living according to an unnecessary law, not living in the freedom offered by Christ. But Paul would encourage the drinking Christian not to make a big deal out of his freedom to drink: don't brag about it, don't argue with the abstainer, and don't drink around him either. Don't let the weaker brother's lack of theological understanding or faith cause division in the church.

Here is what Paul is not saying to the stronger brother: He's not saying, "Since there are alcoholics in your church, you should never drink. You might cause them to stumble." That might in fact be a good principle, but it's not what Paul is saying here. And so to say "Since there are lustful men in your church, you should never wear yoga pants" is a wrong application of the principle in this passage.

In Romans 14 the principle is not about accommodating a brother's sins but about accommodating a brother's lack of theological knowledge or faith in the sufficiency of Christ's work. Just because you understand some spiritual truth your brother doesn't get yet, don't lord it over him or cause unnecessary division in the church because of it. Abide with him as you both continue to grow in faith.

To ask women to apply this principle by making accommodations for a brother's sins, rather than for a brother's lack of theological knowledge and understanding, is a wrongheaded thing to do. That doesn't mean we shouldn't try to love our neighbors through thinking Christianly about our clothing choices; it just means that using this passage to defend that kind of modesty doctrine is inappropriate.

The other verse used to defend the modesty doctrine—really the only verse in the New Testament that links modesty and clothing at all—is 1 Timothy 2:8–10:

I desire then that in every place the men should pray, lifting holy hands without anger or quarreling; likewise also that women should adorn themselves in respectable apparel, with modesty and self-control, not with braided hair and gold or pearls or costly attire, but with what is proper for women who profess godliness—with good works.

The Greek word translated "modesty" here is *kosmios*. This is a word about things being in their appropriate places: it signifies orderliness and self-control. But what was it about braids or pearls that made them inappropriate for Christians worshiping together?

Seminary professor Dr. Sandra Glahn uses Kelly Olson's 2008 illustrated monograph *Dress and the Roman Woman: Self-Presentation and Society* to explain that for first-century women in Ephesus (where Timothy was when Paul's letter arrived), pearls, braids, and clothing were important markers of social status and wealth. While we may think of pearls today as common, in Ephesus, they were real oyster products. While we may think of braids as being childish or unsophisticated, in first-century Europe and Asia Minor, they were a sign of wealth and rank.

"Imagine a head of fine locks wrapped in intricate creations that required slave labor and leisure time (a luxury) to get it 'done' every few days," Glahn writes. "To maintain such a style meant a woman belonged to the ruling or upper class, with the accompanying benefits of power and rank. That is, braids were symbols of rank as much as wealth." Paul worried that women were using their clothes to display their social status and riches. Pearls, braids, and elaborate clothes were "emblems of power. And you don't wear your symbols of power in a place where Jew, Gentile, male, female, slave and free worship together. If you're godly, you're discreet about class."

As Glahn shows, this verse is simply not about sexually suggestive clothing. In fact, were I to use this verse to reprimand a teen visiting my church for wearing a skimpy sundress, I might be doing the exact opposite of what this verse asks me to do; I might be reinforcing class differences rather than working to erase them. A more fitting application of this verse might be to ask people not to drive their Teslas to church or not to come to church draped in diamonds.

Notice that I have used extreme examples here—Teslas and diamonds are truly expensive, often out of the reach of most people I know. I have thus avoided implicating myself and most of my readers. But what if I had said this verse asks us not to wear to church clothing that might have been made by slave labor, or not to carry smartphones, which use minerals also implicated in slave labor, or not to drive new cars or wear cashmere sweaters? In fact, nearly all of us ought to feel implicated by this verse. We tend, in the middle-class churches I've been a part of, to wear our wealth and our social privilege thoughtlessly.

The modesty doctrine of my youth is not scriptural. Modesty in the Bible is more about not flaunting wealth than not flaunting skin. It's possible that the photo I posted today on Instagram, a photo of my feet clad in wool socks that cost $15 and lamb's wool slippers that cost nearly a hundred dollars, was a truly immodest photo. That photo may be far more immodest than a photo of me at a community pool in a two-piece swimsuit. But no one in the church youth group ever helped me think about that.

We might define the modesty called for in 1 Timothy this way: modesty asks a person to be aware of her power—particularly the power of her wealth or social standing—and to refuse to let that power become a cause of division within the church. What is respectable and modest for a woman? To be clothed in good deeds or, as the Bible says elsewhere, to wear God.

This principle could be expanded. Perhaps one's power is not primarily financial. Perhaps it is the power of beauty or education. The call of 1 Timothy 2:9 is for the Christian to make sure she is not flaunting whatever power she has or using it to exclude or oppress others. Instead, she should be using her power for good works. Here, perhaps, one could make a connection to the modesty doctrine I grew up with, the prohibitions about necklines and hemlines. If beauty and the body are sources of power, we ought to consider how to manage that power in ways that are beneficial for the church.

Note two important differences between the way I'm considering the verse now and the way that the youth groups of my past thought about it. First, we're considering culture and context. Knowing what clothing is appropriate is dependent on understanding the cultural context in which it is worn. And, second, the motivation for modesty is different. We're not motivated by a desire to control men or to make accommodations for their sexual urges. Rather, we're motivated by a desire to encourage unity in the church and to help erase oppressive social systems.

If we are defining modesty as becoming aware of one's power

and using it for the common good, one of the potential dangers of practicing modesty remains. The latent danger in practicing modesty correctly is that in trying to avoid parading our power, we might neglect to develop our gifts.

Consider my good friend Matt. In school Matt consistently scored at the very top of his class and in the ninety-ninth percentile in every category on state standardized tests—but he didn't learn this until his midthirties, when sorting through boxes of mementos his parents had saved. His parents never showed him his grades or scores or discussed his intellectual gifts with him. Through junior high, high school, and college, he believed he was of average intellect. Matt's parents wanted him to remain humble and modest; they worried that if they told him how smart he was, he'd become arrogant, or his high achievement would cause division among his siblings. But by trying to help him stay modest, they actually kept him from a healthy kind of self-knowledge. Some of his gifts lay underdeveloped for decades. When he realized this, in his thirties, and finally began a PhD program, he wondered how his life might have been different if they hadn't been afraid. He might have pursued scholarships that would have kept him out of debt. He might have allowed his intellectual curiosity and creativity full rein. It might not have taken him twenty years to figure out where his passions lay.

True modesty does not come from ignoring our strengths. It is impossible to be modest about your gifts if you don't even know you have them! And true modesty does not ask us, once we are aware of our gifts, to pretend they don't exist, to keep quiet about them, to put them in hibernation for a lifetime. I believe this is a common danger for women. Already a broader culture encourages women to downplay their intellect and strength and talent.

When the Canadian newspaper the *Globe and Mail* proposed to change its house style to refer only to medical doctors by their titles, and to use Mr., Mrs., or Ms. for academics who had doctorates, historian Fern Riddell responded on Twitter. She wanted to be identified by her academic degree, not her marital status or gender. Her response caught fire and sparked debate; many men responded to Dr. Riddell, calling her vulgar and immodest. Thus was birthed #immodestwomen, a hashtag used by thousands of women with doctorates who added their titles to their Twitter bios. "You can clearly see that women have been taught to struggle with acknowledging their own authority," Riddell told the BBC in a reported piece the same week, "and the huge backlash . . . online shows how women are taught to know their place."

Is it immodest, having earned a doctorate, to use the title? Perhaps, if you are using it to shame others or to wield your education as a weapon or to exalt yourself at someone else's expense. But that's not what was happening here. Riddell and the women who joined her countered a culture that expects women to define themselves according to their marital status or gender and to keep their strength hidden. Sometimes true modesty will require us, for the good of our neighbors, to be loud, to use our gifts and our strengths in ways that do draw attention to us. Sometimes we need to be angry. It's possible to be angry and modest at the same time; we do this when we use our gifts to counter injustice rather than to prop up existing social structures that divide us from each other.

So when I help my daughter think about how to dress modestly, I am not going to be talking much about hemlines or bra straps. I will not encourage her to keep her intellect and passions hidden so she doesn't intimidate men. Instead, I'll be helping her—and my son—cultivate modesty by thinking about what their gifts are, and what privilege they have, and how they can use all of it to tear down any walls that divide them from their neighbors. If one of our gifts is some measure of disposable income, then rather than buying new clothes, the modest thing to do with it might be to buy some extra food to contribute to the food drive at school this week, or to give it to our church's discretionary fund, to be used in paying electric bills, buying prescription meds, and getting groceries for those in need in our community.

It's possible to be angry and modest at the same time; we do this when we use our gifts to counter injustice rather than to prop up existing social structures that divide us from each other.

Or, perhaps, when I help my daughter think about cultivating modesty, I'll tell her about Elisabeth Elliot's observations when she first lived among the Huaorani. They wore very little clothing—boys wore only a string—but she found they lived together in greater harmony than "most Christians" she had known in the United States. They treated each other with dignity and grace. The Huaorani, Elliot observed, were free from other common sins in the American church, as well—the "vanity, jealousy, covetousness, and discontent which fashion fosters." How much skin is appropriate varies by culture; what does not vary is the truth that we are to treat each other with respect and dignity and use our strengths to serve each other, rather than to separate us from each other.

We can do that wearing almost anything.

CHAPTER 6

AUTHENTICITY

WHEN I WAS FIFTEEN, I WANTED VERY MUCH TO BE REAL. MOST OF US DID then: it was 1996, and we still believed in grunge. We wore flannels and Doc Martens and turned up our noses at anything that smacked of trying too hard, because trying wasn't authentic. We thought social conventions were boring and fake, and that people should just be themselves instead of trying to be like everybody else. In my quest to be real, I eschewed makeup and fashion and pop music. When I came downstairs in the morning to go to school, barefaced, basic, my hair still in the damp braid I'd put it in the night before, my sister, destined to be a successful millennial, would raise her eyebrows and say, "You're not wearing *that* to school, are you?"

We lived in the South, and grunge didn't quite take hold there in the same way it did in other parts of the country—the South was deeply invested in appearance and tradition and civility. In fact, the South seemed to run on appearance, not reality. But I saw myself as different; while most of my peers were talking about the football team, I had a secret crush on the guy who wore the same black shirt to school every day and wrote sarcastic, hilarious essays he'd post anonymously on the bulletin board in the hallway. He was real. And the fact that I liked him rather than the quarterback made me feel real too.

What was harder was figuring out how to be an authentic Christian. So much of Christianity seemed like something someone was trying to sell me. If I could be a good consumer, I could be a good Christian: the right leather prayer journal, the most recent study Bible, the proper bumper sticker. I traveled with my dad to the Christian Booksellers convention one year, and walking the convention floor left me fascinated and nauseated. Christian T-shirts, Christian pencils, Christian romance novels, Christian breath mints, even. What made those breath mints "Christian"? Nothing but the pun in their name (Testa-mints). It seemed everyone there was eager to capitalize on my authentic faith, to turn a profit by using the name of Jesus. None of it felt meaningful. I wanted faith that was more than a marketing ploy.

Maybe it's characteristic of adolescence to obsess about authenticity—but the word was especially in the air as the very last members of Generation X entered high school. The youth pastor at the megachurch I attended shared the larger culture's fixation with generational markers. He'd read all the right research, and he organized our programming around the supposed hallmarks of our generation. In fact, he incorporated an X into everything we did: youth group was Club X, our autumn retreat was XLR8, our Sunday morning service was CrossXroads. We had four key values in our youth group, and banners strung up at the front of "the cave" proclaimed them:

REAL

FRIENDS

XCITEMENT

LIFE

Of course we were real. We didn't want to be hypocrites in any way, especially when it came to faith. We were savvy and skeptical, independent minded, anticonsumerist, true to our true selves. What made our faith real was that we had chosen it ourselves, and we had had deep personal experiences of it. We weren't faking it.

But also it seemed like a lot of us were faking it.

I studied at a private Christian high school, not a fancy one, not the swanky prep school most of my close friends attended, but a tiny, earnest school where we took classes on worldview and read primary sources and had chapel once a week. Our school met in an old shopping mall. We had a handful of classrooms and one larger multipurpose room we called the half-a-caf-a-gym-a-mess-a-torium and used for chapel, theater productions, PE, pep rallies, and lunch. When I think about authenticity, I think about chapel in that room.

One week when we didn't have a speaker for chapel, after

singing a few praise songs, we were invited to "build community" by sharing in that public space a prayer request or something God had been teaching us. As people spoke, my sense that we were all a bunch of phonies grew stronger and stronger. Who would say anything real, anything authentic, anything courageous or vulnerable or honest at all, anything beyond a prepackaged platitude or a prayer request for a distant relative with cancer?

I stood. "Honestly," I said, "I don't have anything to share. I haven't heard anything from God recently. I don't really feel anything. My spiritual life feels pretty dead. So, I guess, pray for me, if you want to."

I sat, a little shaky, feeling brave. Feeling content in my own courageous—and self-righteous—authenticity. I was not playing anybody's game, and I made sure everyone knew it.

Except I was of course playing a game: I was performing my authenticity. I had taken on the role of the girl who didn't care what anybody else thought of her, who was a nonconformist, antimaterialist, always performing her unique individual self. That was just as tiring—and maybe as tiresome—as trying to play by southern society's rules.

/3

Is authenticity a virtue? If to be authentic means to be honest, not deceitful—sincere, not duplicitous—real, not fake—well, then, certainly it is. Honesty and sincerity are good and admirable qualities.

But our cultural definition of authenticity has in recent years grown fuzzier. Now authenticity doesn't mean being true but *speaking your truth.* Someone who is authentic will *tell it like it is,* and we tell each other "You do you." And that is a very different way of defining authenticity.

Take Donald Trump the presidential candidate, for instance. He became known as the "authenticity" candidate but not because he was abundantly honest. Quite the opposite. PolitiFact, the independent fact-checking source, rated Trump midway through his presidential campaign as being truthful only 6 percent of the time and being factually wrong 58 percent of the time. When caught in a falsehood, Trump didn't apologize, but attacked those who sought to correct the record.

Trump was the authenticity candidate not because he was honest and sincere but because he seemed to speak spontaneously. He seemed to speak without preparing remarks beforehand, and this caused him to appear to be a "straight shooter," someone who wasn't playing the DC game, someone who wasn't afraid to hurt people's feelings by telling it like it is.

He couldn't be further from the greasy-haired, thrift store–shopping grunge rockers who embodied that value to me in the nineties. But in 2015 a huge majority of GOP primary voters, 76 percent, told pollsters they believed Trump "says what he believes," rather than saying "what people want to hear."

Columnist Michael Gerson, speaking on *PBS NewsHour,* said Donald Trump demonstrates "a presidential model of authenticity that means thoughtlessness." He appears to speak off-the-cuff, spontaneously, and so people believe he's being honest. He's being real, not pandering to a crowd, and if he gets the facts wrong, well, does that really matter? At least he's being authentic.

White evangelical Americans, perhaps more than most, were primed to respond to just this sort of authenticity. The idea that spontaneous, emotional reaction is more authentic than what is rehearsed sits at the heart of our spiritual tradition.

13

It may seem ridiculous for me to say that white evangelical support of Trump can be explained, in part, by looking at the history of prayer in the Protestant church over the last five hundred years, but I think it's true. Our belief that being spontaneous is more authentic than being rehearsed dates back to theological conflicts of the 1600s.

For hundreds of years Christians had practiced their faith through ritual and liturgy. The pageantry and ceremony of church celebrations and the liturgical calendar were the seasons of life for Christians—they danced around the maypole and celebrated the twelve days of Christmas, baked hot cross buns and lit candles in evergreen wreaths, and often prayed prayers written by somebody else. Faith was something embodied and tactile, something you could smell and taste. It was bending knees and standing tall. It was holy water and bread and wine. And it was practiced in community. The practice of faith was what bound people together. An individual, personal faith was important but not more important than being a part of something larger, being carried along by a current that had existed for generations and would flow into the future in a similar way.

In the sixteenth century, reformers sought to purify the Church of England of all this pomp and circumstance, performance and liturgy.

Reformers rejected both ceremony and liturgical prayer as harmful to the spiritual lives of Christians. Ceremonies and rituals were compromised, they argued—bound up with Catholic superstition as much as with Christian doctrine. Reformers wanted to do away with all rituals: with formal ordination, with wedding rings, with godparents, with "magical" signs or symbols and "hollow" traditions. And liturgy, they said, was repetitive, dull, and an invitation to "perform hypocritically," in one historian's phrase, making it all too easy for churchgoers to speak words that didn't reflect the true emotions of their hearts.

These debates were not waged in cloistered hallways, affecting only a few; they led to civil war. The Church of England had officially broken with the Roman Catholic Church during the reign of Elizabeth I in the mid-sixteenth century, but for the next hundred years, the government swung back and forth between Puritans, who sought far-reaching reform, and the more conservative churchmen who aimed to keep closer to traditional beliefs and practices.

The dispute was resolved with the Restoration of Charles II to England's throne. The reformers lost. In 1662, the Act of Uniformity prescribed the way prayers, sacraments, and other rites of the Church of England were to be practiced. All church ministers would be required to use the new 1662 edition of the Book of Common Prayer when they led worship.

But a small group of English Protestants remained convinced that liturgical prayer was wrongheaded. The only true prayer, they said, was spontaneous, free prayer. For that reason, among others, on an ominous Sunday in August, more than two thousand ministers left the pulpits of the Church of England, never to return. Some of these Puritan nonconformists left for New England, where they eventually formed Presbyterian, Baptist, Methodist, and Congregationalist churches (most American evangelical congregations can trace some part of their heritage back to these reformers). They brought with them a conception and practice of prayer that indexed authenticity to spontaneity.

Like my teenaged Gen-X self, reformers disdained anything that felt like conformity—including liturgy. True prayer, they believed, consisted of unique, spontaneous utterances from the heart.

John Bunyan, known today as the author of *Pilgrim's Progress*, was one such free-prayer advocate. His fear of insincerity was so great he instructed his readers not to pray the Lord's Prayer or to teach it to their children, lest they speak its words without really meaning them.

Instead, he—and others—advocated the spontaneous pouring out of the heart in prayer. That kind of prayer, they said, was evidence of a converted heart and a sincere faith.

But producing spontaneous prayers turned out to be harder than they had anticipated. The self who fled performativity and ritual in prayer found almost instantly how challenging it was to consistently pronounce meaningful personal prayers, and often came up silent and empty. Puritan journals abound with confessions about the difficulty of free prayer. And since free prayer had been linked with sincere faith, difficulty in prayer left Christians wondering if their faith was truly real, after all. Fear of hypocrisy plunged Christians into endless spirals of self-doubt, making assurance of salvation ultimately unattainable. If prayers didn't spring naturally to one's lips, one might question whether one was really saved. And whenever one prayed, a doubt would niggle: Am I being honest? Do I really, sincerely feel the things I'm saying? Are my words an authentic reflection of what is in my heart? Is my faith real, or am I faking it?

To ease anxieties, pastors published books and tracts instructing readers in the art of spontaneous prayer. Their most common solution for achieving true prayer was to memorize lists of phrases, usually from Scripture, in order that one might have at the ready, in Matthew Henry's words, "a Storehouse of Materials for Prayer." And so, paradoxical as it might seem, reformers made new prayer books, as if assembling phrases for the individual to put together was somehow a more authentic form of personal prayer than reading the prayers in the Book of Common Prayer.

But how spontaneous is your speech if it comes from a practiced list of phrases you've memorized? This wasn't spontaneity so much as, in the phrase of literary scholar Lori Branch, *a ritual of spontaneity*. And it's still the way most of us pray today.

Our free prayers today can't be considered spontaneous and emotional and unique and from the heart when they often follow a set pattern. The pattern is obvious to any attentive participant, and a little cynicism inducing, at least to the teen who craves authenticity. At my most cynical, I took to counting the number of "Lord, we just" phrases in people's prayers and mocking the way people used the word *Father* as a filler in their spontaneous prayers. "Lord, we just thank you, Father, for your gifts to us, and Lord, we ask that you would just be with us, God, as we open your

Word this morning, Lord, and listen for the words you're speaking to us, Father."

And who can pretend the words we say before we eat dinner are spontaneous, authentic heart cries when they are so nearly the same every night?

Free prayer isn't wrong, and free prayer that follows a typical form isn't bad. But history has taught us that free prayer is not necessarily more authentic than liturgical prayer. What's important to note here is that several hundred years ago we got authenticity all wrong. When we connected authenticity to spontaneity, and to spontaneous emotional outbursts, that led us to value emotional outbursts over truth. That may be why we fell for Trump's shtick. An appearance of being spontaneous, of speaking off-the-cuff, seemed a sign of authenticity. But if that's authenticity, then forget about it. That's not a virtue at all. I don't want to be "real." I want to be better.

ß

Instead of what we call authenticity, I have come to value masks and costumes, rituals and pageantry and ceremony, what theologian Kevin Vanhoozer calls "the drama of doctrine." If we have any hope of a spontaneous, authentic spiritual expression at some point in our lives, it will only be born of the continual practice of choosing what is loving and right, cultivating the habits of virtue so they may become natural, or second nature. Then, as Plato says, the mask, if worn long enough, may become the face. Or as my grandma used to say, if you keep making that face, it might get stuck that way.

Vanhoozer says that we ought to understand what it means to be a person differently than modern thinkers like Descartes did. When Descartes said, "I think, therefore I am," he implied that to be human was mostly about having a brain—being an independent, disembodied mind whose existence depends on reason. But Vanhoozer argues that to be human is to be a person in conversation with others. I am a "communicative agent" called into existence by God, one "who can enter into dialogical relationship." My selfhood is grounded in my divine creation and calling but exists in and is constructed by my conversations with others. My identity depends on how I respond to my "divine casting call," how I embody the role I've been given, and how I engage with those around me.

I believe I am called to actively live into an identity that is my true one. There is nothing fake about assuming this role—fitting into its costumes, learning its lines, reciting them, or improvising them. Instead, my best chance for authenticity is born from embracing that role. The part I've been called to play is that of disciple, and like a method actor, I must live into the role as best as I can. I can't expect the right response to emerge spontaneously—I have to practice and memorize until, yes, the lines become so familiar to me, like the lines of the prayer book, that I can speak them without even thinking about it.

This will not lead to mindless conformity, but to my unique embodiment of the role. After all, as Vanhoozer points out, both Laurence Olivier and Kenneth Branagh played Hamlet, and played him well. Both inhabited the role effectively but uniquely. Each of us inhabits Christ and is inhabited by Christ in our own distinctive ways.

How do we learn our parts? We study Scripture, allowing our minds to be shaped by the eschatological realities it teaches so we learn to see ourselves and our world correctly. We learn to see how we fit into the drama of redemption. Doctrine strips us of the false masks we give so much time and effort to maintain, allowing us to see ourselves truly as people called, known, and loved by God. Christ is in us (Col. 1:27), and the more we embrace that identity of Christ in us, the closer we come to living authentically.

We also learn our parts by praying, as Vanhoozer writes, referencing C. S. Lewis:

> To pray "Our Father" is to begin to let a new imagination shape our sense of self. To call God "Our Father" is, says Lewis, *to dress up as Christ*. But this dressing up is no play-acting, nor does it have anything to do with hypocrisy. For doctrine directs us to participate in the theo-drama precisely by clothing oneself with "the new self" (Col. 3:10) and putting on the Lord Jesus Christ (Rom. 13:14). Such imagining is no pretense; it is rather a perception of what is actually the case. As Lewis comments: "Very often the only way to get a quality in reality is to start behaving as if you had it already."

So, actually, it's not authenticity I oppose. What can move authenticity from being an adolescent virtue to a mature one is understanding that to be authentic is not to tap some inner well of individuality and spew emotion from there; to be authentic is to practice playing the role I've been given in God's drama until I inhabit it fully—the role of disciple, of one who is in Christ, one who is clothed with compassion, kindness, humility, gentleness, and patience (Col. 3:12). I will inhabit it differently than anyone else, but I don't seek to be unique; I seek to be conformed. When I am conformed to the image of Christ, I am more myself than I could ever be otherwise. And as I inhabit my role more and more fully, my unique performance of it will also shape the broader understanding of what it means to be a disciple; my performance gives the world a fuller picture than it could have without me. As doctrine and ritual shape me, I shape the human understanding of doctrine and ritual.

If this is how I define authenticity, then is it possible for those who aren't followers of Christ to live authentically and virtuously? Of course it is. All people are created in the image of God, so authentic goodness for all of us includes living in ways that affirm the reality of what it means to be human creatures in God's image. Even those who don't believe in God can act in ways that affirm what we know to be true: that life is precious, for example; that we were created for relationships, that meaningful work is a gift, that creativity is part of what it means to be human. When we live in ways that demonstrate these realities, we are living authentically.

To circle back to the original question about spontaneous prayer versus liturgical prayer, defining authenticity this way makes both meaningful. The ritual that might have been empty is not empty if it is performed with the Spirit as practice for the role you are seeking to inhabit authentically. And the anxiety of having to perform spontaneously is gone too; it's okay to just be practicing your lines. Proving your sincerity is not your job; the Spirit in you has made and is making your identity true.

13

How do we help each other remember our true identities and practice putting them on every day? A picture book I used to read to my kids at bedtime, *Nothing* by Mick Inkpen, helps me begin to understand the answer to that question. "The little thing in the attic at Number 47 had forgotten all about daylight," it begins. "It had been squashed in the dark for so long that it could remember very little of anything."

The "little thing" is a faded stuffed animal, left in the attic when a family moves away. As the movers carry boxes out, one points to the animal. "It's nothing," the other says. "Let the new people get rid of it." And so the little thing thinks he has found his identity: he is "nothing."

An encounter with a mouse sparks a memory for Nothing. He sees the mouse's tail and realizes he used to have a tail. Escaping the attic and sliding down a drainpipe, he meets a fox and suddenly remembers he used to have ears and whiskers too. Then a striped frog jogs memories of his own stripes. But as he stares at his reflection in a pond, he finds it odd and ugly. He doesn't recognize himself. He's crying by the pond when a big striped tabby cat lies down next to him. The cat begins to tell Nothing all about himself: his name is Toby, and his family has just moved from Number 47 to Number 97. Nothing recognizes something about the cat but can't name it. Toby volunteers to give Nothing a tour of the neighborhood, and they end up at Toby's new home, trotting in through the back door. He drops Nothing in the lap of an old man dozing in the corner.

When Nothing looks into the old man's face, he instantly remembers who he is and to whom he belongs. "Though he had no ears, nor whiskers, no tail, and no stripes, he was for certain a little cloth tabby cat whose name was not Nothing but Little Toby." Grandpa remembers, too, and pulls out a photo of himself as a baby, snuggling with Little Toby. Grandpa washes him, gives him new ears and whiskers and a tail and stripes, and tucks him in the crib with his grandson.

If I am like Little Toby, unsure about who I am and where I belong, I can't expect to figure it out on my own in the attic, through intense personal soul searching. I figure it out by looking at the world around me—seeing the image of God in my neighbor, the way Little Toby sees whiskers and stripes, and lets them remind him of who he was meant to be. I figure it out by looking into the face of Jesus, like Little Toby looking at the tabby cat; because when we see Jesus, we will be like him, for we will see him as he is (1 John 3:2). I figure it out by letting God stitch me back together and restore my colors, and by abiding in the places where I was meant to be, with the people who are my family. An authentic identity is best cultivated within a community seeking to image God together, to be together where God is.

❦

Around the same time I was reading that book to my kids, Rosie was beginning to learn her alphabet. Letters fascinated her, and I would find her name written everywhere: on our chalkboard, junk mail envelopes, book dust jackets, even the floors and walls.

Her penmanship was distinctive; her *e* looked like a theta (Θ), but it was cute, and I couldn't bear to correct it. She'll learn form and sequence soon enough, I told myself; she will distinguish *b* from *d*, and eventually she will write her *e*'s correctly.

Then, one week, Rosie's teacher at preschool showed her how to form the letter. The girl came home with pages full of *e*, painstakingly traced, repeated over and over again. She came home from school and went straight to her chalkboard to continue drawing them. She seemed to love being shown the right way, being corrected, and practicing the form.

Rosie would never have spontaneously been able to produce an authentic *e*. She needed the repetitive, daily ritual of traceable worksheets. Her dogged perseverance—and joy—in the process inspired me. In those days I was struggling with my own repetitive daily rituals. An adjunct ESL teacher and mother of two preschoolers, I found that the mundane tasks of my life tempted me to mild despair. A prayer I had copied in a decade-old journal became a kind of mantra for me. *Here we are again, Lord, over and over, again and one more time we come before you.* I would breathe this prayer in and out as I went throughout my day. *Here we are again, Lord.* Washing the dishes again. Marking the same grammar mistakes on a load of research papers. *Over and over.* Pulling off Band-Aids. Scrubbing mildew from the crevices around the drain. *Again and one more time.* Walking into the backyard to scream for a quick second. Hoping for a chance to be alone in the bathroom for once. *We come before you.*

I would breathe the prayer in and out, practicing the form, hoping it was forming me.

For a year or two, Rosie would occasionally revert to thetas. The theta-*e* and the backward *R* were what came naturally to her. The true letter shapes, though she knew them, hadn't yet become part of her muscle memory. She had to focus intently to get them right.

Here we are again, Lord, over and over, again and one more time we come before you. The prayer, too, was changing my muscle memory, training my responses toward gratitude and patience. I tried to cultivate thankfulness, but if not that, I at least brought my deformed heart before God, saying here it is, in all its selfish glory, again and one more time. And again, and one more time, God would welcome me and show me who I was made to be.

$$\mathcal{B}$$

As I gain an understanding of true authenticity—an authenticity that consists of "putting on Christ" rather than seeking to bare some sort of internal true self and wondering endlessly if I'm being sincere enough—I have tried to reclaim symbol and ceremony as tools for becoming real. Embracing my identity as a disciple of Christ means rejecting the idea that what is spontaneous is more authentic; it means rehearsal. It means learning the lines, or doctrine, but also learning the blocking—the way to move on the stage, the actions. It means entering a different reality with costume firmly in place and learning how to use props to great effect, how to move in that space and in those clothes.

Around the globe people's spiritual lives are rich with ritual and symbol. Consider the way Muslims pray. At five set times each day, Muslims retreat for prayer. They follow a ritual for purification, use a special mat, face east, and engage their whole bodies, raising hands, bending, and prostrating themselves. Consider the way Sikhs treat their holy book, reverentially waving a fan made of yak hair over the book before reading from it. Or the way Roman Catholics light a candle as they pray, or the way Ethiopian Orthodox remove their shoes when entering a church, reminding themselves they walk on holy ground, or the way Orthodox Christians use icons in worship and wear prayer ropes. The Orthodox prayer rope is worn as a bracelet. Black to symbolize sins, the rope is knotted, so the wearer can finger the knots while praying the Jesus Prayer. This physical symbol is a reminder to pray continually.

Western Protestant churches have some symbols, rituals, and ceremonies: some of us have a cross at the front of the sanctuary, perhaps, and some of us ritually take the Eucharist; we practice the ceremonies of baptism in the water and of donut-eating after Sunday service. But it's worth interrogating our few symbols, rituals, and ceremonies. Are they helping us understand the reality of Christ's kingdom in our everyday lives? Could we make more or better use of them? Are there new ways we could meaningfully incorporate symbols, rituals, and ceremonies into our corporate or individual worship?

My brother John and his wife have done a good job of using rituals and symbols in their family's spiritual life. They have a practice of singing to their children at bedtime and have chosen a song for each child that they sing every night. Sometimes John recites some verses from Proverbs too. During Advent, they set up a tent in their living room and talk about how Jesus "pitched his tent among us" (a literal reading of John 1:14).

When I first started praying for my own babies at bedtime, I wasn't sure how to do it. Ought I to pray spontaneously or use a set prayer from an established source? How was I to model approaching the throne of grace with confidence? What would Rosie and Owen hear when I asked God to grant my requests for them? How could I communicate the truths of the gospel through my prayers so my daughter and son would hear that they were deeply loved but also that they needed grace and God's providential care?

When I prayed, though, the words came almost immediately, without forethought or intention. I prayed they would wake up in the morning with smiles on their faces, songs in their hearts, and joy deep down inside. These were the words I had grown up with— the way my dad had ended every bedtime prayer throughout my own childhood. I thought I had grown up without liturgy, but there they were, the rhythmic words of our family liturgy emerging from the depths of my memory like the truest collect from the Book of Common Prayer.

When my dad prayed every night that I would wake up with a smile on my face and a song in my heart and joy deep down inside, I heard that he loved me and wanted me to be happy, filled with the kind of joy that withstands trying circumstances and is guarded by the peace of God. His love reflected the love of God for me. In this prayer I hope my son and daughter hear that love too. I hope these words, passed down and repeated, help form them into the people God has made them to be—help them find their real, authentic selves.

As we reclaim old rituals, symbols, and ceremonies, and open our-selves up to creating new ones that can enable us to enter more fully into the cosmic reality of the gospel in our present cultural moment, we don't need to worry that we are somehow faking it or being hypocritical. Authentic spiritual engagement does not need to be born of spontaneous emotional expression.

Connecting authenticity to spontaneity several hundred years ago left us with an impoverished sense of discipleship and vulnerable to the appeal of those for whom authenticity is a hollow value. Recovering authenticity as a virtue will mean a fresh embrace of ritual. It will mean acknowledging that we all are performing all the time. The task of the Christian is not to avoid per-formance. Instead, it's to be mindful of what she is performing.

> *Authentic spiritual engagement does not need to be born of spontaneous emotional expression.*

The most authentic Christian is the one who is every day prac-ticing her lines for the role she has been given: sinner, saved by and growing in grace.

CHAPTER 7

LOVE

WE SAT IN A SEMICIRCLE AT A RETREAT CENTER IN THE OZARK MOUNTAINS, huge gray binders on the smooth desks in front of us, pencils at the ready. It was the first day of apologetics camp.

"Before we begin," our teacher said, "we're going to give a few minutes to a researcher who has asked for help with a project."

He introduced Jerry, a dark-haired, bearded fellow in wire-rimmed glasses and a sport coat. "I'm a professor conducting research on the religious beliefs of young people," Jerry explained. "I'd like to ask you all a few questions. First, is there anyone here who is not a Christian?" We looked around the room at each other, high schoolers eager to learn to defend our faith. Nope, no hands were raised. We were all Christians.

Jerry picked one student to address directly. "So you are a Christian," he said. "Why?"

"I think it's the best way of understanding the world?" the student responded tentatively.

"Oh, really?" Jerry looked amused. "And you've studied all possible ways of understanding the world?"

"Well, no." The other students laughed nervously. Jerry pivoted to one of the gigglers.

"What about you? Why are you a Christian?"

The girl stopped smiling.

"Because Jesus saved me," she said.

"Oh, yeah? Saved you from what?" he asked.

"From my sins."

"You're saying that because I haven't been saved by Jesus, because I haven't believed the same fairy tale as you, I'm a sinner going to hell?" Jerry pounced.

She nodded silently.

He got down eye to eye with her and spat out, "You're a narrow-minded, self-righteous bigot!"

The class was quiet.

Jerry stopped role-playing and looked at us, serious and sympathetic.

"That's what may happen when you go to college," he told us. "You are going to face people who are hostile to your faith. The Bible says that we should always be ready to give a reason for the hope that we have. Are you prepared to defend your beliefs when they are challenged?"

Obviously, the role-playing exercise had demonstrated that we were not. Jerry continued lecturing, painting pictures of the kinds of aggressive and offensive behavior we might expect from our college professors. He told us about a sociology professor who had informed a Christian student that if she persisted in believing that abortion was wrong and condoms should not be distributed in middle school, she would have a hard time becoming a social worker; an architecture professor who asked students to try silent meditation; a professor who claimed that communism was superior to any other economic system; a university chaplain who was openly gay; and dorms he'd visited where students did not respond happily to his statement that Jesus was the only way to God.

The solution to these various frightening situations, he assured us, was to be able to give a logical defense of the beliefs we held. It was the only way we would survive.

I should probably confess that I really liked apologetics camp. I went two summers in a row. I loved using critical thinking skills, learning to debate, and getting lost in the woods with smart teenagers who cared about their faith, who were a little geeky, who sought answers to life's mysteries in Mahler and Dostoevsky. I liked some of the teachers better than others, but on the whole they were good people who were interested in art, science, film, and philosophy and weren't afraid of my questions. But instead of teaching me to be curious about the world and open to my neighbors, they taught me to be defensive—to walk through the world expecting opposition, ready to fight until I won my neighbors to my side.

This is the biggest problem with the way I was taught to share my faith—it was defensive and fear based. It wasn't the only problem, of course. It's easy to see now that many of the beliefs we learned to defend were not theological but ethical. The examples Jerry gave to scare us about what we might encounter were only scary if you were coming from a particular partisan position and afraid of any outside influences. That there was a gay chaplain or that it might be difficult to be in social work if you were antiabortion—these were not facts that threatened my belief in God or in God's goodness. Neither were they attacks on me personally or on my faith.

We fail to distinguish between the experience of living in a pluralistic society and the experience of being persecuted for our beliefs. Putting issues such as these—gay marriage, abortion, evolution, gender roles, and political correctness—in our daily study agenda right next to the existence of God and the historical reliability of the Bible is deeply problematic. Perhaps it's not too strong to say that the elevation of ethical positions to essential beliefs has led many people of my generation to leave the church. They aren't

> *People of my generation . . . aren't leaving [the church] because their devious atheist professors got to them but because they saw a church more interested in defending political positions than in loving their neighbors.*

leaving because their devious atheist professors got to them but because they saw a church more interested in defending political positions than in loving their neighbors.

And then there was the problem of logic. The strategies we were taught for defending the faith depended on a set of common beliefs that most people just didn't share anymore. No one I talked to in high school or college was looking for a rational explanation; no one cared about logic. Throughout my college years, I worked regularly with junior high girls. Once, talking with two fourteen-year-olds about their doubts, I said, "Do you think it's possible that two plus two equals four and two plus two equals five could both be true statements?" They shrugged.

"Sure," one said. "Numbers are just something humans invented."

"Same with words," the other added. "Words don't have any real meaning."

I didn't know what to say next. If we couldn't agree that words had meaning, my logical arguments were worthless. What else could I offer?

The strong emphasis on logic was also unhelpful in Southeast Asia, where I went after college. For the most part, those in the East do not share the spirit of logical inquiry that characterized Western thought during and after the Enlightenment. In fact, anthropologist Nobuhiro Nagashima writes that, in the East, "to argue with logical consistency . . . may not only be resented but also regarded as immature." While Westerners argue to determine which of two opposing claims is true and which is false, Eastern thinkers prefer to transcend contradictions, finding truth in both claims. They see reality as not static but dynamic, constantly changing, and so truth, too, is in flux. As Mao Tse-tung put it, "On the one hand [opposites] are opposed to each other, and on the other they are interconnected, interpenetrating, interpermeating and interdependent, and this character is described as identity." Many Asians took a more holistic view of the world than I did.

The apologists who taught me to use the law of noncontradiction as a primary means of defending my faith gave me a tool that might have been useful in Western culture two hundred years ago, but that had little relevance to my generation or to people in the majority of the world's cultures. All the "gotcha" moments I had planned—like where my interlocutor would say, "Truth isn't absolute," and I would retort, "But you've just made an absolute statement!"—disintegrated in my mind. The truth was, no one I met at college was hostile to my faith. I attended a state school with forty-five thousand students. It had a conservative reputation, but I studied in one of the most liberal departments on campus. Still, I never had a professor pick on me because I was a Christian. In fact, my first honors class was taught by a professor whom I saw on Sundays singing hymns across the sanctuary from me. The professors I had who were not people of faith, or who practiced religions other than Christianity, were generally smart, kind, and funny. I admired them. I was open about my faith, and they treated me fairly and decently.

Other students I met weren't hostile to my faith either. Though I'd carefully studied the flow charts offering logical answers to common questions in my copy of *I'm Glad You Asked*, no one ever actually asked me if there was really a God or why I believed in miracles. The evangelistic training I'd received made it hard for me to connect with non-Christians; I found myself always looking for opportunities to drop into our discussions some comment that would lead to a meaningful conversation and, eventually, their conversion. I had no idea how to connect relationally with non-Christians, and in fact I was a bit afraid to. I thought I should only befriend them as a means to win them to Christ. And so I made no real or lasting connections during college with anyone who wasn't already a Christian.

The only way I knew to love people who didn't share my faith was to tell them about Jesus. The only way I knew to fulfill the Great Commandment (to love God and to love my neighbor) was to fulfill the Great Commission (to make disciples of all nations). But somehow evangelism never came across as love; instead, it left people feeling objectified, like the only thing I could see about them was whether they were in or out of God's kingdom. I was unable to see them as fully human, only as minds I might be able to change if I got my argument right. I did not know how to love anyone who was unlike me.

To be fair, the apologetic defense wasn't the only way we evangelicals talked about sharing our faith. We did learn about world religions. I recall pamphlets that unfolded to reveal detailed charts explaining each world religion's take on the vital questions: human nature, God's nature, salvation, the afterlife. But rather than learning about these religions, we learned how to refute them, how to show the superiority of our own.

We also talked a lot about "lifestyle evangelism" and "friendship evangelism." Lifestyle evangelism required us to live such virtuous lives that those observing us would ask, "What makes you different?" But trying so very hard to be good left us inaccessible as people, afraid to show our own weaknesses and failures for fear they might damage our witness. Friendship evangelism was just another way of treating people as objects on a conversion checklist, making friends only with the aim to convert, not with the aim to truly connect. Neither of these methods helped me love my neighbors.

13

That camp, which I attended more than twenty years ago, is still running, and the particular brand of defensiveness and fear it peddled persists among many Christians: fear that we live in a hostile culture.

While attending a conference for Christian families, I listened in on a Q&A session. One worried parent said his oldest child was considering not going to a Christian college. He wanted to know if his kid would be okay at a secular school. "How do we protect our kids from the culture that wants to destroy them?" he asked. Another parent asked how to teach her children to defend their faith against a secular culture that calls for open-mindedness.

Their questions left me stewing in my seat, wishing I could grab the microphone. "There is no monolithic culture out there that wants to eat your child," I'd say. "Stop using the word *culture* that way. And open-mindedness is a pretty good quality to cultivate. Your kids should be curious. If you really believe in the God of the Bible, then you shouldn't be afraid of your kids investigating truth because all truth is God's truth; curiosity will always lead them to God. Your fear and defensiveness, though, might turn them away from Christianity. And remember," I'd say, ending my dramatic monologue with scripture, "God has not given us a spirit of fear" (2 Tim. 1:7 NKJV).

But fear sells; when marketers can feed fear, they can promote products that assuage that fear—books with three-step solutions, conferences with answers, cloistered institutions—and they can profit. Christian institutions have long profited from fearmongering. But Christians are called to love, and perfect love casts out fear.

Perhaps it's worth returning to the one verse always trotted out as a justification for apologetics classes. "Always be prepared to give an answer to everyone who asks you to give the reason for the hope that you have," Peter wrote to "God's elect, exiles scattered throughout the provinces" of Asia Minor (1 Peter 3:15; 1:1 NIV). They were experiencing persecution for their faith. I try to figure out exactly what that persecution looked like, but the biblical scholars I read disagree. Some say it was social discrimination—they were mocked for their faith. Others believe Peter's readers were already facing official discrimination from the government and that 1 Peter 3:15 instructs Christians on how to respond during court hearings. Either way, what is clear is that Peter is not talking about evangelism methods, and he's not encouraging Christians to adopt a combative stance. He's not encouraging Christians to memorize Aquinas's five classic proofs for the existence of God or to courageously contradict their college professors in classes on evolution or existentialism. In fact, he explicitly says our defense of our faith should not be born of fear of the culture. We aren't to argue with those who curse us, but to bless them (3:9). I read the verse in fuller context:

> Who is going to harm you if you are eager to do good? But even if you should suffer for what is right, you are blessed. "Do not fear their threats; do not be frightened." But in your hearts revere Christ as Lord. Always be prepared to give an answer to everyone who asks you to give the reason for the hope that you have. But do this with gentleness and respect, keeping a clear conscience, so that those who speak maliciously against your good behavior in Christ may be ashamed of their slander.
>
> For it is better, if it is God's will, to suffer for doing good than for doing evil. For Christ also suffered once for sins, the righteous for the unrighteous, to bring you to God. He was put to death in the body but made alive in the Spirit. (1 Peter 3:13–18 NIV)

Rather than fighting to maintain a position of cultural dominance, our calling is to embrace any suffering that results from the practice of our faith as suffering that, like Christ's, will bring forth new life.

In context I see Peter telling his readers not to be afraid, but to do good, to honor God, and when people ask, to be willing to explain why their lives are built on hope rather than on fear. The posture of that explanation is as important as the defense itself: Christians ought to speak with gentleness and respect. And rather than fighting to maintain a position of cultural dominance, our calling is to embrace any suffering that results from the practice of our faith as suffering that, like Christ's, will bring forth new life.

13

I'm still terrible at loving my neighbors who aren't Christians. I didn't do it well in college because I was afraid and because I didn't know how to see people as whole people rather than as minds to change. And now, after nearly a decade of working at a Christian college in rural mid-America, the only people I know who don't call themselves Christians are students who are former Christians. And they certainly don't want to hear a logical defense of the faith. In fact, some of them lost their faith precisely because they'd heard one too many logical defenses.

What does it mean to love them? The truth is, I do believe the best way to love my neighbor is to help her see Jesus, but framing love that way isn't always useful. Such a frame suggests there is a disparity between us: I have something she doesn't have, some secret truth, something that always gives me the upper hand. It makes me the teacher, never the student. The answer giver, never the one with questions. But that's not a reflection of reality. I can say that I once was blind, and now I see, but I also have to admit that I don't see everything, and that I need to see the world from her perspective to see it better. As in any healthy relationship, we learn from each other; we change each other. I'm not loving my neighbor as a way to bring her over to my side, to my view of things. I'm loving her because I love her.

Love manifests as curiosity. It's the way my daughter feels about Broadway musicals. She devotes hours to listening to soundtracks, poring over song lyrics, and falling down rabbit holes on YouTube. She can tell you who hosted the 2013 Tonys; she can rap the entirety of Lin Manuel Miranda's "My Shot"; she has memorized choreography to songs from *Newsies*; and for her, Idina Menzel is not primarily *Frozen*'s Elsa but *Wicked*'s Elphaba. Her love expresses itself as curiosity; she wants to learn everything she can about the musicals and the men and women behind them. It reminds me of the way I felt in the first months of my relationship with Jack. I wanted to be where he was, to hear what he was thinking, to know everything about him, from what kind of cereal he ate for breakfast before his first day of kindergarten to what music was playing on his headphones to what he thought about heaven and hell. I still feel that way about him. I want to know about his life, and I want to be there to see it.

My friend Danielle says this is how we should define witnessing. Like me, Danielle grew up in a conservative evangelical home, and like me, she wanted to save the world by preaching the truth of the gospel to her neighbors. But after years of building friendships with Somali Bantu refugees in her neighborhood, she began to understand witnessing differently. The four spiritual laws were irrelevant or incomprehensible to preliterate survivors of war and trauma. As Danielle's curiosity about her neighbors grew, her understanding of her relationship with them changed. Evangelism was less about witnessing through presenting a logical defense of Christianity, and more about being a fearless witness—one who was fully present to the world in all its complexity and pain. Rather than being there to preach to them, she was there to be a witness to their lives: she was someone who saw them.

13

I grew up thinking that loving my neighbor was primarily about caring for her mind and her soul. If I could change her mind, then I could save her from an eternity in hell, and logically, what could be more loving than that?

But these days I'm wondering what it might be like to reimagine neighbor-love using what I've learned of mother-love. I'm beginning to believe that loving my neighbor isn't about having a defense ready, but about letting my defenses down and opening myself up. Jesus said the greatest love is that which lays down its life—that sounds like love that involves the whole body, not just the mind and the soul. And the closest I've seen to love that lays down its life is the love of a woman willing to give her body over to pregnancy and childbirth and the consuming physical demands of caring for another. "The ethos of mothering," poet Cynthia Dewi Oka writes, "involves valuing in and of itself a commitment to the survival and thriving of other bodies." Neighbor-love must be like this mother-love: it is not defensive

Neighbor-love must be like this mother-love: it is not defensive but originates from being unprotected and continues forever in a state of deep vulnerability.

but originates from being unprotected and continues forever in a state of deep vulnerability.

On the Sunday that Owen turned four, he didn't want to go to Sunday school. "I won't get bored in church, Mom, I promise," he said, and slid close to me in the pew, grabbing a prayer book and flipping its pages gently.

Of course he got bored. But he crunched rainbow-colored Goldfish crackers and sat on my lap and hugged me and petted my hair. The rest of the children came in for the end of the service, the baptism, and the Eucharist, and when his sister joined us in the pew, he held a red Goldfish to her lips. "Red," he said, and then instinctively, "the blood of angry men!" *Les Misérables* gave us a moment of Goldfish eucharist. The French Revolution in the mouth of a four-year-old boy in an Episcopal church, a song of sacrifice, a song far too serious for a child who, as far as I was concerned, would never be fighting with his very life for *liberté, égalité, fraternité*.

But I thought of sacrifice again a few minutes later. Owen draped himself across my lap, his neck reclined in the crook of my arm, his legs dangling long over mine, his body far too big to cradle. The feeling of recognition startled me: we were Michelangelo's *Pietà*.

I first saw the *Pietà* when I was twenty, during a semester in Italy. Becoming a mother was the last thing on my mind. But Mary the mother of God was everywhere. I saw her hundreds of times, painted and frescoed and sculpted in museums and churches and gardens. With an angel, with a baby, with a full-grown son. Every time, the Holy Mother left me unsatisfied and confused. She looked so calm. Was she always so sweet, submissive, and docile? Didn't she ever feel confusion? Why did I never see her in pain?

At twenty I could not comprehend why any woman would choose motherhood. Why would you give birth to someone knowing you would inevitably screw him up? Why would you give birth to someone who would steal your heart and then leave you? How could any woman summon the courage to bring into the world a creature who would hurt her, who would be hurt, and who would one day die? *The paintings must be lying*, I thought. It couldn't have been that beautiful. To paint her placid was to deny her great courage in assenting to bear a child, the enormous pain she agreed to open herself up to.

Michelangelo's *Pietà* remains one of my favorites of the Italian Marys. His Mary cradles the lifeless body of the crucified Christ. She is too young to be the mother of an adult man; Michelangelo has made her face smooth-skinned, maybe sixteen, the age she was when she conceived, calm and beautiful and sad. I like how the sculpture brings realities together: the youthful Mary reminding me of the moment new life was announced, the broken body of Christ reminding me of the death that came. Did she know at that age, at the Annunciation, the depth of agony her choice to bear the Son of God would bring to her?

Do any of us ever know what we're getting into when we bring life into the world?

"Motherhood is an open wound," Jessica Mesman Griffith writes to Amy Andrews in *Love & Salt: A Spiritual Friendship Shared in Letters*:

There's new life in me, with a heartbeat. And yet I'm so aware of death! It's no longer a mere possibility but a real thing taking root in my uterus, a being that will live and die. I remember a painting of the Annunciation I saw in the Carnegie Museum in Pittsburgh, the angels coming to Mary with the news. They also carry the implements of Christ's death: the crown of thorns, a nail. Mary tries to shield her eyes, her body. How did she manage to rejoice, to say yes?

I think Mai'a Williams understood better than most women what she was opening herself up to in saying yes to new life. A doula, journalist, poet, and community organizer, Williams says she decided to become a mother after several years of working with Palestinian, Congolese, and Central American indigenous moms in resistance communities. She does not idealize childbirth: "Birth is smelly bloody dirty messy bestial, whether it is vaginal or surgical there is no easy way out. The epidural can ease the pain but not the existential fear." And she does not idealize motherhood, describing the way the experience will inevitably turn you "inside out" and leave you feeling like you can't go on. Mamahood, she says, "is to face yourself and realize that you cannot run away because another life, your child's, depends on this ultimate self-encounter."

She goes on:

I am trying to articulate how the blood and muscle, the tears, the shaking, how it is no longer really a choice, of whether or not you have the courage to not run away from your own fear, panic, lack of self-control. It is something beyond and before courage. It is a visceral sense that vulnerable, quivering life is breaking you and you have to let it. It is not self-sacrifice. It may not even qualify as love. It isn't sweet. It isn't romantic. It may traumatize you, keep you up at night, the memory of that moment when you had to face your worst and best and really you aren't sure if you came out the winner or the loser.

The only word I have is revolution.

I am still waiting for the artwork that shows mother Mary feeling all of this. In the Magnificat, the song Scripture records that Mary sang after agreeing to bear the Son of God, Mary plainly understood that giving birth to Jesus was revolutionary. She saw God scattering the proud, bringing rulers down from their thrones, filling the hungry and sending the rich away empty. God's love, and Mary's love, would upend society. It would change hearts, but also bodies—it would satisfy hungry bellies.

Perhaps what it means to love my neighbor is something like this. Loving my neighbor begins by being unprotected rather than defensive. Loving my neighbor means being open to her in a way that could wound me. Loving my neighbor means giving my body and caring about what happens to her body.

I did not choose to become a mother because I had dealt with all my fears. We say yes to new life not because it's logical or because we understand exactly what it means, not because we believe we are prepared to handle the brilliance of the pain and the complexity of the relationship. We say yes because of love. Our yes means accepting mortality, feeling life and its frailty in our very bones.

And that love bears more love. When nursing, our breasts leak milk at the sound of any baby's cry, not just our own. We've been split open, stretched, sectioned; we've been initiated into the realities of life, blood and filth and salt; and we are forced to live outside of our heads and into earthbound realities. Our hearts now exist outside our bodies, curled up on pews next to us, enlisting in the fight for justice, dying so others may live. To love is to be a little Mary, cradling love too big to hold from the very beginning, cradling it forever with our broken-open bodies, our split-asunder hearts.

13

On one of the last nights of apologetics camp, we always watched a movie. One summer that movie was *Babette's Feast*, and the story it told neatly contradicted everything we'd been taught about the power of the logical, defensive apologetic strategy. Perhaps this was intentional, or perhaps not, but as I look back, I think our teachers knew that loving our neighbors wasn't primarily about winning arguments with them. Maybe the arguments they taught us were more for us and the questions we had than for our neighbors. Maybe that fear Jerry tried to awaken in us with his atheist professor routine wasn't the deepest truth our teachers felt about the world.

Based on a short story by Isak Dinesen, *Babette's Feast* tells of a small village in nineteenth-century Denmark that had forgotten how to desire. The villagers, led by two elderly sisters, follow an austere religious code, and nothing has changed in their village life for many years. One day Babette appears, a refugee from counterrevolutionary bloodshed in Paris. She offers to work as a housekeeper for the sisters in exchange for room and board and cooks for them for the next fourteen years. When she comes into a large sum of money, she invites the whole village to join her for a classic French meal. She spends everything she has on the food: caviar and champagne, quail wrapped in puff pastry and served with *foie gras* and truffles, and on and on. As they move from one course to the next, everyone relaxes; some find long-sought forgiveness, some find romance rekindled, some, finally, admit desire and pleasure into their lives. They begin recalling miracles they'd witnessed and truths they'd learned in childhood. "Remember what we were taught?" they ask. "Little children, love one another."

Babette gave everything she had—including any chance of returning to her old life as an acclaimed chef in Paris—so her friends might feel their hearts open. She never tried to tell them their way of life was wrong; she simply invited them to the table, to desire, and she fed them and awakened their longings.

13

Love isn't rational or defensive or fearful. Love doesn't treat people like objects. Love won't stay cloistered away. Love refuses to win the argument if it will mean losing the relationship. Love sets a table and asks us to taste. Love is curious and brave, and love admits uncertainty. Love looks. Love names our longings. Love asks for everything. Love offers everything. This kind of love is what it means to bear witness and to make disciples.

CHAPTER 8

DISCERNMENT

WHEN I WAS SEVENTEEN, I BECAME A CHRISTIAN EXISTENTIALIST. ADmittedly I was not a normal teenager. Maybe that's not a meaningful category when it comes to teenagers—normal—but consider the evidence: While my friends were at basketball practice, I was reading Camus. While they were eating frozen yogurt on first dates, I was lying on the trampoline in the backyard considering the scientific fact that the stars whose light I could see were already dead. While they were making mixtapes, I was wondering if I really existed. Most people don't give hours of their lives to questions like "How do you know that you know?" But I've always had a tendency to overthink things.

Many nights before I fell asleep, I'd nest in a corner of beige carpet in my bedroom. I'd lean against a pillow propped against the wall, rest my feet on the double bed opposite me, and pull a ragged red spiral notebook from under the bed. Next to me would be my NIV *Student Bible*, black with pink and teal letters on the cover, and probably a bowl of popcorn. I would begin to write my prayers. At the same time, I would process my doubts.

I'd been taught that Christianity was a logical religion, and I wanted it to be. I loved rational argument, and the idea that absolute truth existed offered a measure of security I craved. At church and in my private Christian high school, we read books about the historical proofs for the Bible and the resurrection, and I was all-in. In fact, I sometimes imagined myself as a kind of warrior for truth. For a period of three years—from the end of high school through my first semester of college—when I was assigned essays, I often composed stories instead, stories in which a wistful girl with a glint in her eyes challenged falsehoods wherever she found them. It began when I was supposed to summarize the heresy of Apollinarism and the First Council of Constantinople. What I turned in told the story of a fishy chapel speaker at Peanut Academy whose heresy was exposed by Sophia, an intrepid junior. Peanut Academy, of course, was a stand-in for my own Walnut Valley Christian Academy, and Sophia was the character I wanted to be. I wrote my stories in longhand, black ink or soft pencil on wide-ruled notebook paper.

In her other escapades Sophia had an encounter on an airplane with a cute French existentialist named Luc, chatted in a graveyard with Plato about the nature of reality, and went on college visits where she used C. S. Lewis's *The Abolition of Man* to debate professors about the claims of postmodernism. When Sophia finally enrolled in university, I wrote, postmodernism and its refusal to acknowledge absolute truth would flee.

But my own discomfort with the idea of absolute truth was growing even as I wrote those stories. At night in my journal I'd get tangled up in logic that began to feel circular and unstable. The conversation in my mind would go like this:

A: How do you know that you know?

B: My senses? I come to know reality through what I see and touch and taste and hear and smell.

A: Why do you trust your senses?

B: Because they've proven to be generally trustworthy; what I seem to see seems to also be what other people see.

A: But how do you know the other people are really there?

B: . . .

A: How do you know *you* are even there? How do you know you're not the figment of some god's imagination or a character in someone's dream? Or that you're not like a character in *The Matrix* who took the wrong pill?

B: Well, that seems really unlikely.

A: Based on what?

B: Based on . . . based on my experience of the world.

A: So basically you're saying you know your experience is true because your experience tells you it's true.

Eventually I realized my belief in God depended on my belief that I was real and that I could trust my senses and my brain to apprehend reality and make sense of it. My belief that I was real and could trust my observations depended on my belief in a God who made humans with such capabilities. And so the logic went in circles. There was no way to get outside of the spiral to some ultimate reality, some absolute, undeniable truth. To know anything, I would have to begin by believing something, something ultimately unprovable outside of the system it created.

Maybe your eyes glazed over just reading that. But this is what it meant to me, at seventeen, to say I was a Christian existentialist: it meant that a heroic leap of faith was required if one was to claim to know any truth at all. You couldn't argue your way into truth; at least at the beginning, you had to jump.

Everybody, every single human being, had to begin with some foundational truth they chose to believe, and so I, too, had to make a leap of faith. I could choose anything; it was as intellectually honest to choose to believe in a God who revealed Godself through the Bible and creation as to choose to begin with the presupposition that I could trust my senses or to choose to begin with the belief that the scientific method was the only way to know things or to begin with the belief that love existed.

So how could I choose where to begin? I decided to ask the principal at my Christian high school, who was also one of the teachers who had been letting me turn in Sophia stories instead of essays. He was a careful man who wore tweed and wire-rimmed glasses. To his everlasting credit, he did not laugh at me for overthinking things. Instead, he surprised me: he admitted I might be right. Having faith in God wasn't something that could be justified through pure reason. He suggested that the way to decide what foundational truth to choose to begin with was this: I should choose to put my faith in something that would lead me to a livable life. Maybe discerning what was true, he implied, was a process that wasn't primarily about rational argument but was also about desire, intuition, and the Spirit. Maybe, as Augustine said, we believe in order to understand, rather than understand in order to believe. Maybe I could try out a belief and see how it tasted, see if it was nourishing or noxious.

What he suggested made sense to a girl who had recently rejected the glow of the computer screen for the experience of writing with pencil on paper, a girl who had given up composing essays in an impersonal, authoritative voice in favor of writing stories. I'd already intuited that truth was something best understood through human relationship, narrative, and the experience of my body. But that wasn't something I'd often heard in evangelical culture, which tended to present truth as a set of logical statements delivered by a masculine authority figure for me to accept.

My high school principal actually gave me a more helpful discernment practice than anyone else in my life had. He allowed me to search for truth as a whole person, with a body, mind, heart, and soul, rather than just as a brain. He told me to let my doubts seek answers not just in logic or an external authority, but in my desire. I doubted that God was real; but I didn't want to live without God. A life without God was not, for me, one that was livable—it would lead me to despair. And so my desire led me to belief.

Desires, shaped and led by the Holy Spirit, can be a part of our practice of discernment. This is not to say that whatever I want must be true and good because I want it (as the pastor of the church I attended in college said when he left his wife and children, claiming he had never known God's joy with them the way he had known God's joy with the other woman). And this is not to say that desire is a more perfect guide to truth than reason or the Bible or the authority of church tradition; it is only to say that trying to find truth without paying attention to desire is like trying to prepare dinner without owning any knives. It can be done, maybe, but it severely limits what you'll be able to serve.

Desires play a role in discerning truth—this is, perhaps, why the psalmist instructs us to "taste and see that the LORD is good" (Ps. 34:8). Ángel Méndez-Montoya, a professor of theology, philosophy, and cultural studies in Mexico City, argues that knowing is a form of savoring. He points out that, in Spanish, the words are related:

> The etymology of both *saber* (to know) and *sabor* (to savor) is rooted in the Latin *sapio* or *sapere*, meaning to taste, to have a flavor, as well as to understand. *Sapientia*, later translated into English as wisdom, means to have knowledge or wisdom of the world, but also to taste things in the world. Likewise, the word *sapiens* means being wise, and it is also derived from *sapere*, to taste and/or to know.

The kind of knowing that comes through bodily experience has been devalued in contemporary evangelicalism. Influenced by the

Western philosophical tradition (initiated by Plato and Aristotle), we have tended to regard touch, smell, and taste as the lowest forms of knowledge exactly because they originate in the body. Perhaps not coincidentally, the Western tradition has long associated women with emotions and the body, and men with logic and the mind. But the kind of knowledge that comes from the body is not subordinate to the kind of knowledge that comes through mental reasoning; they work in tandem, and if one is subject to the other, the practice of the Eucharist may suggest that it is taste that rules.

The kind of knowledge that comes from the body is not subordinate to the kind of knowledge that comes through mental reasoning; they work in tandem.

Méndez-Montoya quotes philosopher Lisa Heldke to illustrate the knowledge that comes from the body:

> The knowing involved in making a cake is "contained" not simply "in my head" but in my hands, my wrist, my eyes and nose as well. The phrase "bodily knowledge" is not a metaphor. It is an acknowledgment of the fact that I know things literally with my body, that I, "as" my hands, know when the bread dough is sufficiently kneaded, and I "as" my nose *know* when the pie is done.

In this same way we can come to know the truth about God through the experiences of our bodies.

If one way to know what is good and true is by tasting it, maybe good eating practices can help me think about good discernment practices. The way chef Andrew Zimmern describes the American diet sounds an awful lot like the Christian diet I grew up on. The host of several travel and cuisine television shows, Zimmern has built a reputation by eating foods that seem bizarre to Americans. He argues that we're actually disposed to like most foods—it's culture that teaches us that some things are gross. He has tried to avoid such language in raising his son. By the time Zimmern's son was four, he'd eaten almost everything he was offered, from bats to dung beetles. But one day, when digging in the garden together, Zimmern asked his son if he wanted to eat an earthworm, and his son grimaced and said it was gross to eat worms. Shocked, Zimmern investigated and found that his son had a picture book that had taught him "Candy is yummy, but worms are yucky."

Zimmern argues that Americans have a "messed up view" of food. We're spoiled, and we've let convenience dictate our food habits. This is bad for our health, and it's also bad for the earth: "If we keep eating the same 15 vegetables, the same four meats and the same three fish, we're going to create more of an extinctive forecast for ourselves than we're already dealing with." Labeling some foods as "yucky," he says, is immature and dangerous.

Cultural ideas about what is disgusting have limited our ability to enjoy a wide range of foods, and the repercussions may be dire not just for us, but for the planet. I see the same kind of limited appetite among Christians when it comes to developing our taste for truth; we read the same fifteen authors, listen to the same four preachers, and sing the same three praise songs. Anything beyond the familiar we label gross. I remember this kind of mocking language passing for discernment in my childhood—driving past a church marquee with a woman pastor's name on it and laughing about how it wasn't a real church if it had a woman leading it. Or making up chants about Democratic presidential candidate Michael Dukakis being a cockroach, when we had no idea what he stood for, just a sense that he was gross.

Our limited diet is leaving us undernourished and our ecosystem weakened. If we want to be able to taste and enjoy God's truth, we have to stop labeling as gross or heretical those things that are new or strange—or common on the other side of the world but not in our neighborhood. God invites us to move from a limited diet to a rich and surprising one. We will be healthier, and so will our communities, if we lose our fear of the unfamiliar and taste new things.

To develop a better palate, we need to move from junk food to slow food—from nutrient-light, artificial foodstuff to food that requires preparation. For me this means making sure that when I'm trying to know what's true, I don't just reach for what's convenient, for a quick and easy answer. I need to take time. I practice reading things that require extended focus, texts that are difficult and complex and those that are old as well as new. I read the mystics. I try silence and meditation. I slow myself down with these things when I find myself too quickly jumping to conclusions about what is true; when I've been reading Twitter for too long, I take a break and read Julian of Norwich instead.

I also practice ordering what other people order. Like the droll diner in *When Harry Met Sally*, I say "I'll have what she's having" whenever I see someone who seems to know how to delight in what is true. I copy them. I read the books they cite in their endnotes, and I hang around the places they hang around, and I go on walks with them—and as I figure out how they see the world, my own understanding of what is true grows deeper. This becomes even more fun when I try to copy people who are very different from each other. Odd pairings explode with flavor, and in these weird combinations, I taste things I've never tasted before. It's discernment as fusion dining, as diverse tastes come together to help me develop a better palate.

I don't think that expanding your palate for truth always means moving outside of or away from your spiritual community, though. In fact, for me, it's pretty important to eat with the same people every week, to have space where conversations can continue for years with people I know down to my bones—people unafraid to disagree with me. These are the conversations where we practice loving the truth by being willing to gesture toward it as much as we can, in humility and in acknowledgment of mystery. This is not easy to do. We have one example of how to attempt it in Jewish tradition.

In *The Burning Word: A Christian Encounter with Jewish Midrash*, Judith Kunst describes how observant Jews are taught to study the Bible, paired off into *hevrutot*, or study friends. Starting as young children,

> they gather in the *bet midrash*, or study house, in a group of
> ten or twenty or a hundred to hunch in pairs over open Bibles,

perhaps with the same partner they've had since youth. (The *hevruta* relationship is so important that the Israeli army takes pains to assign childhood *hevrutot* to serve in the same combat units.)

Half the students read the Torah portion aloud while

the other half of each pair listens intently . . . then jumps in with a response, thus commencing an intense, often hours-long session of questioning, answering, arguing—a robust, communal exploration of a text which, tradition holds, God commands them to interpret.

This whole system embraces and relies on debate. Participants expect to disagree, but that doesn't hinder the discussion—it furthers it. At times study friends will make mistakes and follow faulty paths of interpretation. They may say something offensive. But their discourse goes on because it happens in the context of relationship. These disagreements are always personal; they do not take place between disembodied strangers online (as ours often do), but with intimate friends. Study friends also make sure to position their debates within historical context as they use commentaries written by thinkers and theologians through the ages.

This is a high-stakes conversation, Kunst writes, "where not just the text on the table but also the multiple arguments over what it means are considered sacred, vital to the religious life of everyone in the room, of the entire community, and of the entire nation of Israel." Rather than freeze in fear over making a mistake, for these devout Jews, "it may be more important to be in conversation with each other and get it 'wrong' than to get it 'right' but have the conversation stop."

The goal of *hevrutot* is to continue the conversation. It's worth noting that the word conversation partners use for the scripture they're studying is not *passage* but *portion*. Scripture isn't something to get from one side of to the other, something to pass through on your way to certainty—though that's often how we treat it in Christian Bible studies. The word *portion* implies something else—that Scripture feeds us, that the language is to be savored, chewed, and ingested. We can learn from the example of the *hevrutot* that loving truth may be more about delighting in Scripture together than about getting through a passage of Scripture to the right answers.

♫

The research of food psychologist Paul Rozin shows that Americans have a particularly bad attitude toward food: we are consumed with anxiety about fried foods and fat content, and compared to the Japanese, the French, and the Belgians, we worry more about what we eat while also being more likely to consider our eating habits unhealthy. Rozin believes we have lost touch with the pleasures of eating and that forgetting pleasure is a form of self-harm.

I think we have lost touch with the pleasures of the truth. Fear of the unfamiliar and a desperate need to have certainty and to be right have limited our ability to taste and see that God is good. It's not that we don't need to be careful about what we allow to enter our minds and hearts and bodies. We do need to be careful but not in a fearful way—in a thoughtful and attentive and inquisitive way. Maybe even with relish and joy. If something tastes good, ask why. If Rush Limbaugh or Stephen Colbert tastes right to me, why is that? Is it a sign that there is truth there, or is it a sign that my biases are being tickled? If I'm not sure, maybe I can ask someone else to help me discern, maybe someone who I know will disagree with me. And if I'm eating the same thing every day, I need to be aware of what that means for my health—which nutrients I'm missing, what flavor profiles I might be losing my ability to taste.

I know taste is subjective. But while absolute truth exists, we can't pretend it is absolutely knowable or communicable. We are subjects. We are subject. None of these practices of discernment—not rational argument, not the very best Bible study, not listening to church authority, not remaining in community, not learning from diverse voices, not attending to our bodies and emotions and what delights us—can get us to absolute truth.

My own journey in understanding how to seek truth began with the realization that reason couldn't lead me to it. And yet I've written this whole chapter employing reason to dethrone reason, using words to suggest that words can't capture truth. Maybe I should have told a story instead. Maybe I should have told a story about Sophia, who went to college and realized that postmodernism had some pretty valid critiques of the Enlightenment tendency to treat truth like a butterfly to be caught, pinned, and studied. Sophia learned, instead, to see truth as a butterfly to follow, to see how it looked different from spring to fall, from meadow to mountain, to see how it stayed the same whether she was tired of following it or filled with enthusiasm, to see what else could be learned about the butterfly when traveling with different people in its pursuit.

Or perhaps we should have gone on a walk or shared a meal or opened the Scriptures together and prayed.

Ángel Méndez-Montoya says that "from a eucharistic account, taste reigns supreme among the senses, and takes a primacy over the intellect, becoming a foretaste of the beatific vision." This resonates with me. Taste takes primacy over the intellect because truth is not a set of statements but a person, a person who said, "I am the truth," and who said, "I am the bread of life," and who brought me to his banqueting table and gave me himself to eat. The more I eat that bread, the more I desire it, and the sweeter it tastes. I can't fully communicate the truth with words, but I can eat the truth, and when I do, it becomes enfleshed in me.

So we keep setting the table with good things. And we keep talking. And we keep listening and inviting more people to eat with us. And we believe that in that never-ending feast, the Holy Spirit will lead us into all truth.

CHAPTER 9

HOPE

I DIDN'T BUY THEM BECAUSE I LOVE ANIMALS OR BECAUSE I COULDN'T resist the soft butteriness of their fluffy new-chick down. I didn't buy them because of the tiny hops they took with tiny feet or the way they looked up at me and cheeped. I didn't buy them because I was hungry or to please my children. It happened like this: my son and I were grocery shopping and had an extra twenty minutes before it was time to pick up his sister from preschool. So we stopped at the farm supply store to look at the animals.

We live in rural Indiana, as foreign a country as any place I've ever lived (and I've lived in four different countries). When Jack and I moved here, the first thing we noticed was the way women wore bikinis on their riding mowers; I loved their fearless body positivity.

If the weather is nice, people drive their golf carts into town to buy ice cream, and on Labor Day they drive them from house to house at our all-town garage sale. The 3,700-person town is famous for an ice cream shop called Ivanhoe's, though newspapers say the best thing to order is not the ice cream but the pork sandwich: tenderloin, pounded thin, heavily breaded, and fried, served with lettuce on a white bun.

In the summer you'll see adolescents walking to the gas station, walking home with Styrofoam cups of soda, 44 ounces for 69 cents. Boys uncomfortable with their sudden growth spurts hunch to be shorter, leaning toward girls with ponytails like corn silk, and I wonder about these girls—whether they dream of college or of being Corn Queen, carrying red roses in a convertible in the Labor Day parade, or both.

Near the end of our third winter here, we bought a house on two acres of land just outside the city limits. Leaving our rental house in town meant we could raise chickens, if we wanted to, and have space for a garden and bees, fulfilling our idyllic Wendell Berry–fueled fantasies. Raising chickens is not a dream most townspeople here share; residents have outlawed chickens and other farm animals within the four square miles of town. While my citified friends in Denver and Little Rock and Seattle happily experiment with urban chickens in their backyards, locals here are the children of farmers: they are already intimately familiar with the noise a rooster makes at 4:00 a.m., the way hens cackle after laying an egg, the mess, the way hawks and weasels and coyotes—even cats—will attack. They know you might need a gun.

But I bought our chicks while we still lived in town, reasoning they'd stay in the garage for the first six weeks anyway, and no one would know I was breaking the law. I bought them because I was beginning to believe spring would never come; the wait for winter to end had begun to seem interminable. After all, I'd grown up in San Antonio, where we decorated our Christmas tree while wearing shorts and T-shirts, and lit a fire in the fireplace if the temperature dropped into the fifties. On Easter we couldn't hide hard-boiled eggs in the outdoor Easter egg hunt because it was too hot—they'd begin to smell. In Indiana, Easter passed, and the snow refused to melt.

I had been cold for a full six months. The land lay barren and hard, the sky hovered gray and close, and my will to get out of bed shrank. Evening wear transitioned seamlessly into day wear as I added furry slippers and a hoodie to the leggings and loose long-sleeved tee I slept in and padded to the kitchen to make coffee. My desires were disappearing. Even my favorite indulgences failed to excite me. I'd as soon eat the frozen pizza as the braised short ribs, and I could take or leave the glass of Malbec. Instead of writing or lesson planning, I would brew French press after French press of coffee and read Twitter as if it had a point. I sat in front of my happy light and took vitamin D, but nothing made me angry, nothing stirred my imagination, and I didn't even want to want.

So when I finally wanted something—baby chicks—I bought them. They were the visible manifestation of my belief that spring would come.

13

We might say that hope is the virtue of believing that spring will come and acting accordingly. Spring is, of course, metaphor; spring is life rather than death. Spring is heaven and the return of Jesus and abundance and fecundity and flowers and babies (and spring chickens) and love. But spring as metaphor is not specific enough to be helpful in understanding how to practice hope. We believe in the springlike triumph of life over death; sure, that sounds pretty, but what does it mean? What will it look like, and how do we practice hoping for it?

For me, Christian hope used to mean that we who had put our faith in Jesus would be rescued from this late, great planet Earth and taken up to heaven with God while those who had rejected God would be subject to eternal conscious torment in hell. Only two things will last, I was taught: the Word of God and the souls of men. Everything else will burn. If that was true, then the way to practice hope, to anticipate the future I longed for, was to study the Bible and try to convert others to Christianity, and maybe have some babies since they would have souls and could be converted too. Nothing else ultimately mattered. I shouldn't care about the trees or the oceans or the ever-growing list of endangered species. I could feel free to exploit earth's resources since they would burn eventually anyway. I oughtn't try to make anything beautiful, to write a poem or a song, to make a painting or a quilt unless the artwork could be construed as evangelistic, as potentially encouraging nonbelievers to believe in Christ. Everything narrowed to a gnostic hope in the immortality of the soul.

But what if that was the wrong hope? What if, instead, Christians ought to hope that all things will be made new—to believe that when Paul says that all creation groans, waiting for the children of God to be revealed, he's reminding us that the gospel isn't just a story about the "souls of men." Instead, it's a story about a whole world in bondage to decay and a whole world that will obtain the "freedom of the glory of God." What if, rather than expecting to be raptured to some home in the clouds, I ought to expect that Jesus will do what he said he would do: he will return to earth—this earth—and he will marry it to heaven. His kingdom will come here.

If this is my hope, then the way I practice hope changes. Evangelism and Bible study can still be part of my practice, but so can gardening and writing poems, bringing order to messy account books, teaching preschoolers to shape the letters of their names, even raising chickens. Practicing hope means seeking justice, caring for the earth, making and celebrating beauty, awakening others to curiosity about their lives, and proclaiming through these actions that God is God, that death and corruption don't win, that despite all evidence to the contrary, every part of this world is precious, and rescue is on the way.

13

Our move-in date was pushed back by two weeks; the snow began to melt, and the birds grew too big for the box in the garage. I moved the chicks, little down-covered softballs, to the backyard, closing them into the storage shed overnight. The neighbor girls, including the cop's nine-year-old daughter, came to play with our pets. They named them: Duke (the rooster), and the hens, Goldie, Calico, Queenie, Star Bright, and Nightmare.

One afternoon I realized Queenie was gone. I scoured the street for her, but it wasn't until that night, when my husband came home, that we found a pile of yellow feathers fifty yards behind the house.

What to tell the kids? We worried, worried, then simply told them the truth, unadorned. A hawk had probably eaten Queenie. My daughter—who had carried the chicks in her hands and on her shoulders, who had fed and watered them daily, who loved them—just nodded, as if death was a natural part of life.

↗3

We call girls *chicks* and *mother hens*, and say women get as *mad as an ol' wet hen*. Arrogant men are *cocksure*, and whoever *rules the roost* is the *cock of the walk*. These gendered English idioms express centuries-old sentiments. Aristophanes called the cock the ancient sovereign of Persia, while the Roman writer Pliny praised it for its bravery, declaring roosters to be "sentinels and astronomers" whose fighting prowess awed even lions. The hen was never likened to the ancient sovereign of Persia.

The wild red jungle fowl of India, the forebear of our domesticated chicken, was first captured by the Burmese, and not for food, but for sport. (Cockfighting, in fact, is the longest-running sport in the world, with a 3,500-year history, and was still legal in Louisiana up until the last decade.) The Burmese exported the red jungle fowl to China, but officials almost immediately made it illegal to raise the birds for food. Perhaps the Chinese worried that the presence of humans would contaminate the chickens.

The Romans had no such fear. Archaeology indicates that

big, organized farms in Rome provided the first chance for large-scale chicken production. Farmers fattened their flocks with bread soaked in wine or milk or mash made of cumin seeds, barley, and lizard fat. Again the government became involved: out of concern for excess and gluttony, the Roman consul Gaius Fannius ordered that households could eat only one chicken per meal.

After the fall of Rome their industrious methods of raising chickens fell out of use until the beginning of the last century, when technological developments in chicken feed allowed Americans to begin raising hens exclusively indoors, in cages. In the hundred years since chicken farming in America ceased being primarily a casual, local enterprise—half a dozen birds in the side yard of the house, scratching for worms in the dirt—and became a thriving industry, chicken has become the American meat of choice. We now consume nine billion birds per year.

My mother came to visit when we moved into our house in the country, bringing a wrought-iron rooster. "I thought you might want it on your front porch," she said. "It's so cute." The rooster, in contemporary mythology, is still powerful, arrogant, beautiful: the cock of the walk, the one-time emblem of the Democratic Party, an animal worthy of front porch display.

The hen, the female of the species, we have turned into a protein-producing commodity, feeding her high-calorie food so tempting that she refuses to go outdoors even when the outdoors is offered, preferring to stay near the feed trough. She's bred to get breasts so large that her legs break under her. Most often her five weeks of life pass in a building with twenty thousand other broilers, in a cage where she doesn't even have room to spread her wings. Not once.

13

Jack built a chicken coop on our new property, but we let the birds range freely during the day, feeding them store-bought chicken feed to fortify their foraged diet of worms and weeds. I'd chosen a mixture of breeds based on a friend's advice: all docile, friendly birds, good for egg production. Duke and Nightmare, Australorps, have shiny black feathers. Goldie is the only Orpington now that Queenie is gone, a classic yellow bird, and Callie and Star Bright are Golden-Laced Wyandottes, every stunning copper-colored feather on their bodies edged in black.

At the end of the summer, the chickens were nearly five months old, which meant they'd already lived about five times as long as most chickens raised in the United States for consumption. But we were not raising ours for meat: they're for eggs, and they began laying small, orange-yolked eggs for us at the end of September.

This was also about the time we realized we did not want a rooster.

We hadn't planned to get a rooster—they were all supposed to be hens—but it's hard to tell with chicks, and some roosters always get into the mix at the farm supply store. Now we'd had him for almost five months, and I was torn: Duke was loud, yes, but he was also protective, chasing the cat away from the hens. On the other hand, we were paying to feed an animal who would never produce any food for us. He didn't lay, and we wanted layers. After a week or two of deliberating, my gentle, kind husband decided to slaughter him.

This was not a casual, throwaway decision. It was born out of years of trying to be more aware of what we eat: of not eating factory-farmed meat, of memberships in CSAs that provided local and organic vegetables and fruit, of experiments in small-scale gardening. It was born out of books we'd read, out of Wendell Berry and Michael Pollan and Barbara Kingsolver. It was a symbolic gesture that would stick it to the food industrial complex, that would say we refused to be disconnected from the reality that animals must be slaughtered in order for humans to eat meat.

YouTube research indicated that slaughtering a chicken was not difficult. The calm, measured voices of men on videos instructed us to prepare a milk jug by trimming the plastic from the top and bottom and attaching it upside down to the edge of a table. Simply hold the bird upside down, and the flow of blood to its brain will cause it to go limp. Slip the head through the milk jug, then slit the throat. The blood will flow out in the vessel you've prepared to catch it. Pluck and cook.

Jack's experience was not so smooth. Duke was spooked and ran around the garage like a chicken with its head cut off long before his head was actually cut off. Being held upside down did not cause him to fall into a trance or to relax; he was frantic, pecking at Jack's arms, angry. His head did not fit in the milk jug.

I can't tell you what happened, finally, because Jack doesn't like to tell the story, and I wasn't there. But an hour later he returned to the house, pale. "It's done," he said.

COQ AU VIN

Ingredients:

6 slices bacon, chopped

Legs and thighs of a rooster

Medium onion, diced

2 carrots, roughly chopped

5 cloves garlic, minced

1 pound white mushrooms, sliced

2 tablespoons butter

2 cups cabernet

Instructions:

Sauté bacon in a large cast-iron skillet over medium low heat until fat is rendered. Remove bacon from the skillet and set aside. Increase heat to medium.

Salt chicken pieces, then place fat side down in skillet and cook until both sides are golden brown. Remove from pan and set aside.

Sauté onions, carrots, and garlic in bacon grease until onions are translucent, about 5 minutes. Remove with slotted spoon and set aside.

In a separate skillet, sauté mushrooms in 2 tablespoons butter until golden, about 3 minutes. Set aside.

Pour the wine into the cast-iron pan, whisking to loosen any bits that have stuck. Simmer for 3 minutes, then add rest of ingredients: bacon, chicken, onion, carrots, garlic, and mushrooms. Lightly salt. Cover and bake at 350 degrees for 75 to 90 minutes.

GOAT CHEESE POLENTA

Ingredients:

4 ¹/₂ cups water

1 cup polenta

Salt to taste

2 tablespoons butter

4 ounces goat cheese

Instructions:

Bring 4 ¹/₂ cups water to a boil, then slowly add 1 cup polenta, whisking continuously. Simmer gently for ten minutes. Salt to taste. Add two tablespoons butter and four ounces goat cheese. Stir until combined.

To serve this meal, spoon generous helpings of the gravy atop the polenta. Put a leg and thigh on each plate. Take the food and two glasses of red wine to the basement, where the television is. Put on a movie while you enjoy your dinner.

Cut into the dark meat of the rooster, Duke.

Carefully lift the meat to the side of the plate, enjoying the carrots, onion, bacon, gravy, and polenta, when you realize that you will not eat him. Enjoy the flavor he's lent to the gravy, be thankful for his life, for the five months he roamed freely. Save the rest of his carcass to make stock for soup.

Become a vegetarian for the next two weeks.

After dinner I escape the mess and noise of my kitchen with a plate of table scraps for the girls. "Here chickie chickie chickie," I call, like all ancient farm wives have called. The hens run toward me, bouncing from foot to foot.

I shouldn't give them table scraps this often; it makes them discontent with their normal feed, but I don't care: it saves money, and it means less goes to waste. There is great beauty in the way that on our small homestead nothing is ever wasted. When I clean out the coop, the hay and mess go into the compost with other kitchen and garden scraps. The compost goes into the garden, making our dense, claylike soil both lighter and richer. The nutrients feed the arugula and corn and tomato plants, which feed us. And any leftovers feed the chickens. The chickens give us eggs, and they eat the mosquitoes and ticks in the yard, and they leave fresh fertilizer in their coop. It's a beautiful cycle, when it works, when it's not interrupted by predators or insects or drought or floods or frost or curious cats or the chickens eating their own eggs, leaving nothing but empty shells for me to collect.

Maybe it's true that being connected to the whole process—birth, life, death, seed, soil—can help us recover a sense of our own humanity. Maybe it's true that raising chickens in the backyard rather than in industrial chicken farms is better for them and for us, but it's still far from idyllic. It still leaves us all at the mercy of nature.

Sometimes I wonder if the cultural shift—what Wendell Berry calls "cultural amnesia"—about what it means to eat animals contributes to a more general confusion about what it means to be human. Are we becoming as likely to see women as commodities as we are to see chickens as commodities? A few years ago a young man in California killed six women because they refused to have sex with him. What about American culture had led him to believe that women are objects, commodities, things he should be able to touch and use at will? Why did he believe that his life was meaningless if he couldn't possess the women he wanted to possess? How did he grow to see women like factory-farmed chickens, purposefully plumped and packaged, cut into legs, thighs, breasts?

I think about him as I feed the chickens in the evenings. Knowing Nightmare, Star Bright, Goldie, and Callie, I can no longer view the shrink-wrapped breasts in the grocery store in quite the same way. Had he never known any women as women, as individual persons? Had he only ever seen them as consumable parts?

The world is not yet right, factory, farm, funeral. Sometimes we eat our own.

↗3

Jesus compared himself to a chicken. I had a vision of this passage in my mind: the man standing alone, or maybe with his disciples, on a hill overlooking the city, contemplating its history and its present, then murmuring to himself, "O Jerusalem, Jerusalem, the one who kills the prophets and stones those who are sent to her! How often I wanted to gather your children together, as a hen gathers her chicks under her wings, but you were not willing! See! Your house is left to you desolate" (Matt. 23:37–38 NKJV).

That's not how it happened though. He was standing in front of a large crowd of followers and disciples, preaching. It was just after his triumphal entry into Jerusalem, all palm branches and praise, and his shocking cleaning of the temple, turning over the tables of the money changers. He'd been healing and preaching with authority, decrying the hypocrisy of the scribes and Pharisees.

And then this man, with his sinewy carpenter arms, calloused hands, and dirty feet, stopped, overcome with compassion for the people in front of him. And he didn't say, "How often I would have fought for you like a lion." He didn't say, "How often I would have annihilated your enemies and hidden you in my castle."

He said something that, try as I might, I can't imagine my brother or my husband or my dad saying, full of emotion, in front of a large group of people. *To* a large group of people, he compared himself to a mother hen. With the knowledge that he was the next of the "sent" ones to be killed for coming to the rescue, and even knowing how they would turn against him in the next few days, he longed to gather them like a mother hen under his wings, clucking, feathering, settling in to be the safe place in the straw where the chicks could hide.

He wished to restore his self-absorbed, rebellious, hard-hearted people to himself, these murderers of the prophets, these people who looked at the world with eyes that could not see it for what it was or what it would someday be. "*How often would I have gathered thy children together, as a hen doth gather her brood under her wings, and ye would not!*" (Luke 13:34 KJV, emphasis mine).

Hope, I begin to believe, does have something to do with feathers. Hope is being willing to find shelter under Jesus' wings.

⅓

The chickens' first winter was also the harshest winter Indiana had known in twenty years.

The temperature didn't venture above freezing for weeks, and the same hard snow muted the landscape for twenty-seven days. Everything outside was white, whipped into submission by a bitter wind and spitting snow, and once again I felt myself losing hope. It wasn't exhaustion or depression but what Kathleen Norris calls acedia: "the death-in-life that I know all too well, when my capacity for joy shrivels up and, like drought-stricken grass, I die down to the roots to wait it out." I suffer from it every winter when the new year arrives, yet nothing feels new.

When the windchill dipped down to the negative forties, we brought the hens into the garage, but other than that, they survived for several months in their coop with a single heat lamp. Extreme winds in an early spring storm blew the roof straight off their coop, but in the morning they were all still there.

When I had been cold for half a year, tired of waiting for change, I decided I had to do something. I found myself again looking for some tangible action I could take to prove that winter would, in fact, end, that spring would someday come. That year—instead of chicks—I turned to vegetable seeds. If faith is the evidence of things unseen, then maybe seed catalogs are the evidence of spring. I pored over the beautifully illustrated, richly described advertisements for plants. I spent two hundred dollars on seeds and starts. Seeds! The moment the ground thawed, I borrowed a tiller and turned the soil, thirteen hundred square feet of it. Mud clumped to the blades of the machine, but I pulled it off with my hands and kept going. The hens came over and pecked in the dirt for worms I'd turned up, leaving fresh fertilizer in the tilled soil.

I was in way over my head: more seeds than I could possibly keep straight, too much garden space to care for, and yet still not enough to accommodate all my wintry dreams. I accidentally killed a batch of seedlings under heat lamps in the garage. I left town for a conference and let the weeds and grass reseed themselves in the ground I'd tilled but never cleared. I hauled wood home in the minivan with my two small children and convinced my husband to build raised beds. Bare-root strawberry plants arrived in the mail—twenty-five of them—and I had no space prepared. I killed weeds by covering them with cardboard. I planted tiny seeds.

Spring descended on all my mistakes, and vegetables grew: arugula, chard, lettuce, and peas. I rode the mower across our two acres in my tankini, defiant. A little jubilant. I chose to believe that nothing is ever wasted, that there is a God who sees neither women nor chickens as commodities, who watches us and weeps for us and will not rest until things are made right. I chose hope, believing that my seedlings and my hens are signposts for another world, one where every broken part has been repaired, where every old thing has been made new, where we remember what it means to be human, where we are all finally, finally gathered like chicks under a mother's wings.

ACKNOWLEDGMENTS

I WAS PRIVATELY CONSIDERING TURNING ALL MY CREATIVE ENERGIES FROM book writing to amateur quilting—in other words, giving up—when I told Lauren Winner about my idea for this book. "Well, if you decide against writing it," she said at the end of our conversation on a windswept day on Whidbey Island, "you can give the idea to me as a Christmas present." Lauren, your faith gave me faith, and your generosity made every chapter better. I don't know whether to call you coparent or midwife of this book. I'm most grateful to call you friend.

My agent, Ross Harris, is a wonder-worker. Thank you for plucking me from The Millions and making your magic happen.

From the first moment I spoke with my publisher, Daisy Hutton, I knew that she understood my lament and my hope. I'm grateful for the way she and the whole team at W Publishing Group have supported me.

Many people offered helpful feedback on portions of this book, including Suzanne Paola, Sarah Sanderson, Cara Strickland, Laura Neale, Abi Noble, John Noble, Beth Bowman, Anna Kendrick, Kendall Vanderslice, Katie Walker, Jim Warnock, Stina Kielsmeier-Cook, Kelley Nikondeha, Danielle Mayfield, and Christiana Peterson. Jessica Goudeau read portions but, more importantly, delivered bossy pep talks and carpool-line last-minute edits in my moments of need. I'm grateful to the Collegeville Institute and my workshop group there, especially Catherine Ricketts; my Reimagining Virtue colloquium, especially Heidi Davis; and the women of Greenlake Presbyterian Church, especially the brilliant Blythe Adamson. Special thanks to those who read an early draft in its entirety: Mollie Fitzpatrick, David Lepine, and Bob Lepine.

I'm grateful to the students and friends who bravely allowed me to share their stories.

I'm grateful to Rachel Held Evans, who believed in this book. Rachel, your radical inclusivity, tireless advocacy, and consistent promotion of others' voices made the publishing industry and the American church better. We miss you.

Every idea in this book grows from the communities that have nurtured me in the last decade. I'm thankful for my parents and my siblings, our ridiculous group texts; for my writing group, their solidarity and encouragement; for Gethsemane Episcopal Church in Marion, Indiana, and all my friends and colleagues there; for the Ockenga Honors scholars, who ask questions and are willing to be surprised by the answers; for the Saturday morning book club, women who fight to hang on to faith and to end misogyny in the church; and for the Sunday night soup crowd of spring 2019, who set an example of abiding with people who don't always know how to love you.

Rosemary and Owen, your compassion, creativity, humor, and courage inspired me as I wrote this book. May you grow rooted and established in love so that you may have power together with all the saints to grasp how wide and long and high and deep is the love of Christ, and to know this love that surpasses knowledge—that you may be filled to the measure of all the fullness of God.

Most of all, I'm grateful to Jack, my heart's companion, my partner through apocalypse, the best proof I've found that grace exists.

NOTES

INTRODUCTION: VIRTUES FOR THE APOCALYPSE

xv **"I won't have any soup today":** Heinrich Hoffman, "The Story of Augustus, Who Would Not Have Any Soup," in *The Book of Virtues*, ed. William J. Bennett (New York: Simon and Schuster, 1993), 45.

xvii **in support of Trump:** Some examples of this hypocrisy:

Ralph Reed, founder of the Christian Coalition, on Bill Clinton, 1998: "Character matters and the American people are hungry for that message. We care about the conduct of our leaders, and we will not rest until we have leaders of good moral character" (Laurie Goodstein, "The Testing of a President: The Conservatives," *New York Times*, September 20, 1998, mobile.nytimes.com/1998/09/20/us/testing

-president-conservatives-christian-coalition-moans-lack-anger
-clinton.html).

Ralph Reed, on release of the *Access Hollywood* tapes in
which Trump was heard discussing forcing himself on women,
2016: "I just don't think an audiotape of an eleven-year-old
private conversation with an entertainment talk show host on
a tour bus, for which the candidate has apologized profusely
[note: he hadn't], is likely to rank high on the hierarchy of
concerns of those faith-based voters" ("Faith Leaders Are
Still Backing Trump in Wake of His Lewd Comments About
Women," NPR, Weekend Edition Saturday, October 8, 2016,
https://www.npr.org/2016/10/08/497164715/faith-leaders-are
-still-backing-trump-in-the-wake-of-his-lewd-comments-about
-wom).

Dr. James Dobson, founder of Focus on the Family,
discussing Bill Clinton in a letter to about 2.4 million
supporters, 1998: "What has alarmed me throughout this
episode has been the willingness of my fellow citizens to
rationalize the President's behavior even as they suspected,
and later knew, he was lying" (Goodstein, "The Testing of a
President").

Meanwhile, Dobson, when in late April 2019 the
Washington Post tallied Trump's count of false or misleading
claims while in office at 10,111, has remained silent about
the lies. In fact, he also called on his supporters to pray that
President Trump would not be impeached (Lauren Gill,
"Trump Impeachment Must Be Prevented Through Day of
Fasting and Prayer, Evangelist Says," *Newsweek*, January 9,

2018, newsweek.com/trump-impeachment-must-be-prevented
-through-day-fasting-and-prayer-evangelist-775333). Granted,
Dobson is no longer the head of Focus on the Family. That
role is now filled by Jim Daly, who—as far as I can see—has
also not spoken publicly about Trump's dishonesty. On his
blog, *Daly Focus*, on November 9, 2016, he posted a reflection
titled "Why I Am Encouraged by the Prospect of a Trump
Presidency."

However, others who worked at Focus on the Family who
publicly criticized Trump in their personal writing or on social
media faced direct consequences, as the *Atlantic* reported in
February 2017 (Emma Green, "These Conservative Christians
Are Opposed to Trump—and Suffering the Consequences,"
Atlantic, February 11, 2017, theatlantic.com/politics/archive
/2017/02/conservative-christians-disagreement-trump/516132).

Franklin Graham, president of the Billy Graham
Evangelistic Association and Samaritan's Purse, discussing Bill
Clinton's sins, 1998: "But the God of the Bible says that what
one does in private does matter" (Franklin Graham, "Clinton's
Sins Aren't Private," *Wall Street Journal*, August 27, 1998,
wsj.com/articles/SB904162265981632000).

Franklin Graham, on Trump, 2018: "Trump's affair with
Stormy Daniels is 'nobody's business'" ("Billy Graham's Son:
God Put Trump in Office," video interview, Associated Press,
May 3, 2018, youtube.com/watch?v=F-oFJULEWxM).

xviii **willing to overlook it:** The *Washington Post* reported on the
growing acceptance of politicians' immoral behavior: Philip
Bump, "The Group Least Likely to Think the U.S. Has a

Responsibility to Accept Refugees? Evangelicals." *Washington Post*, May 24, 2018, washingtonpost.com/news/politics/wp /2018/05/24/the-group-least-likely-to-think-the-u-s-has-a -responsibility-to-accept-refugees-evangelicals/?noredirect =on&utm_term=.c3ddcf8b83a3.

xx   **can help build empathy:** David Comer Kidd and Emanuele Castano, "Reading Literary Fiction Improves Theory of Mind," *Science* 342, no. 6156 (October 18, 2013): 377–80, doi.10.1126/science.1239918.

xxii   **discouragement and faith:** Miriam Schulman reviewed the book for *Ethics*, a publication of Santa Clara University: Miriam Schulman, "Moral Literacy: The Virtue of *The Book of Virtues*," review, *Issues in Ethics* 7, no. 1 (winter 1996), Santa Clara University, legacy.scu.edu/ethics/publications/iie /v7n1/bennett.html.

xxiv   **Lament is the seedbed of hope:** I think this phrase originally comes from Walter Brueggemann.

xxv   **"our culture, our history, and our traditions":** The publisher's description for *The Book of Virtues* says that "these stories are a rich mine of moral literacy, a reliable moral reference point that will help anchor our children and ourselves in our culture, our history, and our traditions—the sources of the ideals by which we wish to live our lives."

CHAPTER 1: LAMENT

5   **readings we hear most often:** For the statistics about how many psalms of lament are used in various denominational liturgies, see Denise Hopkins, *Journey Through the Psalms*

(St. Louis: Chalice, 2002), 5–6, and Lester Meyer, in "A Lack
of Laments in the Church's Use of the Psalter," *Lutheran
Quarterly* (Spring 1993): 67–78. Meyer wrote:

> The lectionary for Sundays and major festivals appoints
> psalms to be read over a three-year cycle; frequently these
> are cited in longer and shorter versions, the latter described
> as appropriate when sung between lessons at the Lord's
> Supper. There are also psalms appointed for other holy days
> and special occasions, as well as a "Daily Office Lectionary";
> these will not be included in our analysis because, despite
> a strong tradition of daily worship in Anglicanism, most
> Episcopalians (like their Lutheran counterparts) tend to limit
> their attendance at worship to Sundays and major festivals.
>
> The Episcopal lectionary's three-year cycle omits sixty-
> seven psalms. Of these, twenty-nine are individual laments (3,
> 4, 5, 6, 7, 9, 10, 12, 28, 35, 38, 39, 41, 52, 55, 56, 57, 59, 61,
> 64, 77, 88, 94, 102, 109, 120, 140, 141, 143) and eight are
> community laments (58, 60, 74, 79, 83, 108, 129, 137). Thus,
> 55 percent of the omitted psalms are laments. When one adds
> to this total the eleven psalms (11, 14, 30, 49, 53, 73, 75, 82,
> 106, 115, 144) that are related to the laments, the percentage
> rises to 72 percent.

7   **begin to understand it:** My understanding of lament is
    shaped by Lauren F. Winner's exploration of the practice in
    The Dangers of Christian Practice (New Haven, CT: Yale
    University Press, 2018); Denise M. Ackermann's *After the*

Locusts: Letters from a Landscape of Faith (Grand Rapids: Eerdmans, 2003); Walter Brueggemann's *The Prophetic Imagination* (Minneapolis: Fortress, 1978) and *Peace* (St. Louis, MO: Chalice, 2001); Leslie C. Allen's *A Liturgy of Grief* (Grand Rapids: Baker Academic, 2011); Soong-Chan Rah's *Prophetic Lament: A Call for Justice in Troubled Times* (Downers Grove, IL: IVP, 2015); and Kathleen O'Conner's *Lamentations and the Tears of the World* (Ossining, NY: Orbis, 2002).

10 **"vision of survival and salvation"**: Walter Brueggemann, *Peace* (St. Louis, MO: Chalice, 2001), 27.

10 **"proper management and joyous celebration"**: Brueggemann, 27.

11 **a chance to embrace vulnerability:** This is how theorist Judith Butler describes the moment of missed opportunity in the United States in the wake of 9/11: We who were at the top, who were usually invincible, had the reality of our vulnerability exposed. We had two options in responding. We could mourn together and allow our shared grief to fuel a shared outrage—to entrench our sense of ourselves as ones who ought to be invulnerable and to lead to violence and retribution. Or we could mourn together but instead reflect on our injuries and "find out who else suffers from permeable borders, unexpected violence, dispossession, and fear, and in what ways." Rather than doubling down on our myth of independence, we could "begin to imagine a world in which that violence might be minimized, in which an inevitable interdependency becomes acknowledged as the basis for global political community."

Perhaps it's too idealistic to imagine that a nation might

be able to respond to tragedy in this way, to imagine that any political body could choose vulnerability and interdependence when "self-sufficiency and unbridled sovereignty" are woven into its identity. But maybe it's not too idealistic to imagine that when followers of Jesus experience deep grief, we could allow that experience to deepen our understanding of the suffering that others have experienced.

Quoted material is from the preface (page xii) to Judith Butler's essay collection *Precarious Life: The Powers of Mourning and Violence* (Brooklyn, NY: Verso, 2004).

13 **seventeen months of pregnancy**: Tahlequah's story was widely reported in 2018. Lori Cuthbert, Douglas Main, "Orca Mother Drops Calf, After Unprecedented 17 Days of Mourning," National Geographic, August 13, 2018, nationalgeographic.com/animals/2018/08/orca-mourning-calf -killer-whale-northwest-news/.

14 **"in alphabetical order"**: Kathleen M. O'Connor, *Lamentations and the Tears of the World* (Ossining, NY: Orbis, 2002), 11.

15 **"even as suffering eludes containment"**: O'Connor, 13.

15 **"confidence in God and in the future"**: O'Connor, 14.

15 **"renewal and restoration"**: Leslie Allen, *A Liturgy of Grief* (Grand Rapids: Baker Academic, 2011), 148.

18 **"Weeping permits newness"**: Walter Brueggemann, *The Prophetic Imagination* (Minneapolis: Fortress, 2001), 57.

CHAPTER 2: KINDNESS

22 **Janet Soskice**: I am indebted to Lauren Winner for introducing me to Janet Martin Soskice and *The Kindness of God*

(New York: Oxford University Press, 2007) through her book *Wearing God: Clothing, Laughter, Fire, and Other Overlooked Ways of Meeting God* (New York: HarperOne, 2015).

23 **"the rock which is our salvation"**: Soskice, *Kindness of God*, 5.

26 **"versus 2 percent of black families"**: Bethany Romano, "Racial wealth gap continues to grow between black and white families, regardless of college attainment," Heller School, Brandeis University, July 16, 2018, heller.brandeis.edu /news/items/releases/2018/meschede-taylor-college-attainment -racial-wealth-gap.html.

26 **"much more common"**: Romano.

27 **"closing the racial wealth gap"**: Romano.

30 **Isa. 56:6–8**: My understanding of Isaiah 56 is informed by the work of Kelley Nikondeha in her book *Adopted: The Sacrament of Belonging in a Fractured World* (Grand Rapids: Eerdmans, 2017), 130.

31 **erased rather than entrenched**: Read about Jubilee in Leviticus 25, Deuteronomy 15, Isaiah 61, and Luke 4.

33 **"members of the same family"**: These thoughts from Kimmerer come from her brilliant essay on the subject, "Speaking of Nature," in the March/April 2017 issue of *Orion*, https://orionmagazine.org/article/speaking-of-nature/.

34 **"children at Carlisle?"**: Kimmerer, "Speaking of Nature."

35 **all created beings**: Randy Woodley's *Shalom and the Community of Creation: An Indigenous Vision* (Grand

Rapids: Eerdmans, 2012) has shaped my thinking on the Christian response to the natural world.

36 **"or not at all"**: I'm grateful to my husband, Jack, for introducing me to Donna Haraway's *Staying with the Trouble: Making Kin in the Chthulucene* (Durham, NC: Duke University Press, 2016), from which these snippets are taken.

37 **within the decade**: Darryl Fears, "One Million Species Face Extinction, U.N. Report Says. And Humans Will Suffer as a Result," *Washington Post*, May 6, 2019, washingtonpost.com /climate-environment/2019/05/06/one-million-species-face -extinction-un-panel-says-humans-will-suffer-result.

CHAPTER 3: HOSPITALITY

49 **made my way home**: I first told the story of encountering Leigh in *Dangerous Territory: My Misguided Quest to Save the World* (Grand Rapids: Discovery House, 2017).

50 **openness to strangers**: Christine Pohl, *Making Room: Recovering Hospitality as a Christian Tradition* (Grand Rapids: Eerdmans, 1999).

51 **white evangelicals agreed**: Hannah Hartig, "Republicans Turn More Negative Toward Refugees as Number Admitted to U.S. Plummets," *FactTank*, Pew Research Center, May 24, 2018, pewresearch.org/fact-tank/2018/05/24/republicans-turn -more-negative-toward-refugees-as-number-admitted-to-u-s -plummets/.

52 **thirsty and imprisoned**: My argument here is informed by Pohl, *Making Room*, 19, 28.

54 **led a campaign**: The campaign was summarized on The Justice

Conference website, www.thejusticeconference.com/2018/05
/need-know-families-separated-border/.

55 **outside your group:** I teach about in-group bias in my
Intercultural Communication class. The concept has been
around at least since 1906, when William Graham Sumner
wrote about it in *Folkways*. In *Racial and Ethnic Groups*
(London: Pearson Education, 2012), Richard Schaefer argues
that in-group bias can manifest in "in-group virtues" and
"out-group vices"—the behaviors of one's in-group are seen
as naturally virtuous, and the behaviors of the out-group are
perceived as unacceptable.

55 **blind and hard of heart:** While the field of epigenetics is a new
one, several studies indicate that trauma can cause genetic
changes that are passed down. See, for example, Olga Khazan,
"Inherited Trauma Shapes Your Health," *Atlantic*, October 16,
2018, theatlantic.com/health/archive/2018/10/trauma
-inherited-generations/573055/.

57 **no longer a stranger:** These insights into Lydia's story come
from Arthur Sutherland, *I Was a Stranger: A Christian
Theology of Hospitality* (Nashville: Abingdon, 2006).

CHAPTER 4: PURITY

66 **"Purity of Heart Is to Will One Thing":** In 1938, Danish
philosopher Søren Kierkegaard published an address titled
"Purity of Heart Is to Will One Thing" to encourage Christians
to approach the confession of sin without ambivalence.

69 **"'sexual abstinence' refer to":** Thanks to Abi Noble for
pointing me to Tina Schermer Sellers. Here I quote from her

Sex, God, and the Conservative Church (Abingdon, UK: Routledge, 2017), 2, 10–11.

74 **overcome the emotional response:** This experiment is discussed in Richard Beck, *Unclean: Meditations on Purity, Hospitality, and Mortality* (Eugene, OR: Cascade, 2011), 23.

74 **American evangelicalism:** Beck, 48.

75 **dependent on culture:** Beck, 16.

80 *Mein Kampf:* Adolf Hitler, *Mein Kampf*, trans. Ralph Mannheim (New York: Houghton Mifflin, 1943).

80 **religious minorities, among others:** The use of purity language among members of Pol Pot's regime is documented in Hurst Hannum, "International Law and Cambodian Genocide: The Sounds of Silence," *Human Rights Quarterly* 11, no. 1 (February 1989).

80 **those coming to the United States:** See, for example, "Preventing Crimes Against Humanity in the US," *The Conversation*, June 22, 2018, theconversation.com/preventing -crimes-against-humanity-in-the-us-98679; and Abigail Simon, "People Are Angry President Trump Used This Word to Describe Undocumented Immigrants," *Time*, June 19, 2018, time.com/5316087/donald-trump-immigration-infest/.

81 **obedience to the Deuteronomic law:** Deuteronomy 23:3 says, "No Ammonite or Moabite or any of their descendants may enter the assembly of the LORD, not even in the tenth generation" (NIV). In Ezra 10 and Nehemiah 13, the men called for all Moabites to be expelled from Israel based on this law.

82 **the nature of God:** John Dominic Crossan calls Ruth a "challenge parable" in *The Power of Parable: How Fiction*

by *Jesus Became Fiction about Jesus* (New York: HarperOne, 2012). My thoughts here are also influenced by the *Wisdom Commentary on Ruth* written by Alice Laffey and Mahri Leonard-Fleckman (Collegeville, MN: Michael Glazier–Liturgical Press, 2017).

Scholars debate whether the book of Ruth was written in the pre-exilic or the post-exilic period. Whether or not the book was originally intended to challenge the reforms of Ezra and Nehemiah, it's fair to say that Ruth's full inclusion as part of Israel indicates that ethnic purity is not the primary characteristic of the people of God.

It's also important to note that Ruth is not a romantic fairy tale; it's a story of God showing Godself to be faithful to Naomi, who is a kind of female Job character, through the great sacrifices made by Ruth and Boaz. For more on this, please see *The Gospel of Ruth: Loving God Enough to Break the Rules* (Grand Rapids: Zondervan Academic, 2011).

83   **in the wrong place:** Douglas even finds that this definition of purity explains the Levitical laws about "clean" and "unclean" animals. Animals that were unclean were those which didn't wholly conform to their class, which were in some sense out of place.

84   **"in the place of excrement":** From his poem "Crazy Jane Talks to the Bishop" (*The Winding Stair and Other Poems*, 1933).

85   **characterized by unity:** See John 17.

CHAPTER 5: MODESTY

91   **"discontent which fashion fosters":** Elisabeth Elliot reflected on this experience some years after it in *The Liberty of Obedience* (Ann Arbor, MI: Servant, 1968), 17.

97   **wealth and rank:** Sandra Glahn's commentary can be found here: "Not with Braided Hair . . . or Pearls," *Engage*, December 14, 2010, https://blogs.bible.org/engage/sandra _glahn/not_with_braided_hair...or_pearls__.

98   **"discreet about class":** Glahn.

99   **to wear God:** Lauren Winner explores the implications of Paul's statement in Galatians 3 that we ought to clothe ourselves with Christ in her book *Wearing God: Clothing, Laughter, Fire, and Other Overlooked Ways of Meeting God* (New York: HarperOne, 2015).

101   **marital status or gender:** See this BBC report on Dr. Riddell: Patrick Evans, "'It's Dr, not Ms,' Insists Historian," BBC News, June 15, 2018, bbc.com/news/uk-44496876.

103   **"discontent which fashion fosters":** Again, from Elliot's *Liberty of Obedience*, 17.

CHAPTER 6: AUTHENTICITY

109   **factually wrong 58 percent of the time:** John Baldoni, "Is Donald Trump a Role Model for Authenticity?" *Forbes*, January 2, 2016, forbes.com/sites/johnbaldoni/2016/01/02/is -donald-trump-a-role-model-for-authenticity/#6ce8d5d833bc.

109   **"what people want to hear":** A *New York Times*/CBS poll in 2015 commented on in the *Washington Post*: Greg Sargent, "Who Is the 'Authenticity' Candidate of 2016? Yup: It's

Donald Trump," *Washington Post*, December 11, 2015, washingtonpost.com/blogs/plum-line/wp/2015/12/11/who-is -the-authenticity-candidate-of-2016-yup-its-donald-trump /?utm_term=.31a60cf1f0f6.

109 **"authenticity that means thoughtlessness":** "Shields and Gerson on the Biggest Political Moments of 2015," *PBS*, January 1, 2016, pbs.org/newshour/show/shields-and-gerson -on-the-biggest-political-moments-of-2015.

110 **prayers written by somebody else:** For a historical account of the role of prayer books in the lives of early Americans, see "People of the Book" in Lauren F. Winner, *A Cheerful and Comfortable Faith: Anglican Religious Practice in the Elite Households of Eighteenth-Century Virginia* (New Haven, CT: Yale University Press, 2010).

111 **true emotions of their hearts:** In this section I'm summarizing an argument made by Lori Branch in *Rituals of Spontaneity: Sentiment and Secularism from Free Prayer to Wordsworth* (Waco, TX: Baylor University Press, 2006). I am indebted to Lauren Winner for directing me to this book.

113 **"Materials for Prayer":** Matthew Henry published *A Method for Prayer* in 1710. In the introductory note to the reader, he used these words to describe the contents of the book.

113 *a ritual of spontaneity:* Branch, *Rituals of Spontaneity*.

114 **"the drama of doctrine":** Kevin Vanhoozer, *The Doctrine of Drama: A Canonical Linguistic Approach to Christian Theology* (Louisville, KY: Westminster John Knox, 2005); see esp. chap. 11.

115 **"dialogical relationship":** Vanhoozer, 367.

115 **"divine casting call"**: Vanhoozer, 368.

116 **"behaving as if you had it already"**: Vanhoozer, 394.

118 **he is "nothing"**: Mick Inkpen, *Nothing* (London: Hodder & Stoughton: 1996).

119 **in the crib with his grandson**: Inkpen, *Nothing*.

CHAPTER 7: LOVE

128 **won my neighbors to my side:** The strict dividing lines young evangelicals were taught to see between who was in and who was out, who was with us and who was against us, have contributed to the polarization of today's political and religious climate. Our apologetics lesson didn't teach us to listen to those who were different from us but only to defeat their arguments. So the evangelicals now calling for us to #emptythepews of churches that don't fully align with our beliefs are, in fact, enacting the same kind of fundamentalist response they were taught when they were evangelical children: those who are not with us are against us. We aren't here to listen to them, but to shut them down. On both sides the need for total purity in ideological agreement ends the possibility of meaningful engagement or personal change or love.

130 **view of the world than I did:** These ideas, including the quotations from Nagashima and Mao Tse-tung, come from Richard Nisbett's *The Geography of Thought: How Asians and Westerners Think Differently . . . and Why* (New York: Free Press, 2003), chap. 7.

136 **to understand witnessing differently:** In *Assimilate or Go*

Home: Notes from a Failed Missionary on Rediscovering Faith (New York: HarperOne, 2016), D. L. Mayfield tells the story of how her relationships with Somali Bantu refugees changed her understanding of what it means to witness.

137 **"of other bodies"**: Cynthia Dewi Oka, "Between the Lines," in *Revolutionary Mothering: Love on the Front Lines*, ed. Alexis Pauline Gumbs, China Martens, and Mai'a Williams (Oakland, CA: PM Press, 2016), 52.

140 **"to say yes"**: Amy Andrews, Jessica Mesman Griffith, *Love & Salt: A Spiritual Friendship Shared in Letters* (Chicago: Loyola University Press, 2013), 196.

140 **"ultimate self-encounter"**: Williams, from sec. 5 introduction, *Revolutionary Mothering*, 148–49.

141 **"only word I have is revolution"**: Williams, 148–49.

143 **awakened their longings:** David John Seel, in his book *The New Copernicans*, studies how millennials see the world. He argues for an "apologetics based on desire," one that captures imaginations with a vision of flourishing and that addresses the human longing for justice, spirituality, relationship, and beauty. "The mission of the fellow pilgrim in the lives of these haunted New Copernicans is to affirm their longings and to point them to a relationship that adds to and completes these longings. . . . Christianity is the answer to a real existential longing. Its interpretative power is not found in a philosophical argument so much as in the living of life and particularly living in the midst of one's deepest longings." David John Seel Jr., *The New Copernicans: Millennials and the Survival of the Church* (Nashville: Thomas Nelson, 2018), 155.

CHAPTER 8: DISCERNMENT

150 **"to taste and/or to know"**: Ángel F. Méndez-Montoya, *The Theology of Food: Eating and the Eucharist* (Hoboken, NJ: John Wiley & Sons, 2012), 46. I am indebted to Kendall Vanderslice for directing me to this book.

151 **"when the pie is done"**: Lisa Heldke, quoted in Méndez-Montoya, *Theology of Food*, 52–53.

152 **"worms are yucky"**: Andrew Zimmern wrote about his son and the earthworm for *Time*: "Andrew Zimmern Explains How to Acquire a Taste," *Time*, February 5, 2016, time.com/4187760/andrew-zimmern-acquiring-taste/.

152 **immature and dangerous**: Zimmern, *Time*.

155 **"commands them to interpret"**: Judith M. Kunst, *The Burning Word: A Christian Encounter with Jewish Midrash* (Brewster, MA: Paraclete, 2006), 39–40.

156 **"the conversation stop"**: Kunst, 39.

156 **a form of self-harm**: Paul Rozin was quoted in Kat McGowan, "Food: The Science of Scrumptious," *Psychology Today*, September 1, 2003, psychologytoday.com/us/articles/200309/food-the-science-scrumptious.

158 **"foretaste of the beatific vision"**: Méndez-Montoya, *Theology of Food*, 47.

CHAPTER 9: HOPE

162 **Everything else will burn**: For example, Chuck Swindoll: "Do you realize there are only two eternal things on earth today? Only two: people and God's Word. Everything else will ultimately be burned up—everything else. Kind of sets your

priorities straight, doesn't it?," Charles R. Swindoll, "What Lasts Forever? Only Two Things," from the article library of the Bible-Teaching Ministry of Charles R. Swindoll, July 8, 2015, insight.org/resources/article-library/individual/what -lasts-forever-only-two-things.

163 **His kingdom will come here:** My understanding of Christian hope is informed by N. T. Wright's *Surprised by Hope* (New York: HarperOne, 2008).

165 **only one chicken per meal:** Learn more about the history of chicken farming in Andrew Lawler and Jerry Adler, "How the Chicken Conquered the World," Smithsonian.com, June 2012, www.smithsonianmag.com/history/how-the-chicken-conquered -the-world-87583657/.

170 **"cultural amnesia":** From Wendell Berry's essay "The Pleasures of Eating," originally published in *What Are People For?* (New York: North Point, 1990).

173 **"to wait it out":** Kathleen Norris, *The Cloister Walk* (New York: Riverhead Books, 1997), 130.

ABOUT THE AUTHOR

AMY PETERSON IS A WRITER AND TEACHER WHOSE WORK HAS APPEARED in the Millions, *Washington Post, Other Journal, Cresset, Christianity Today, River Teeth, Christian Century,* and elsewhere. She is the author of *Dangerous Territory: My Misguided Quest to Save the World.*

For more information, please visit
amypeterson.net